Dec, 2019

The Reflection Connection

Reflecting and Connecting to Life's Experiences

Gary R. Gasaway

Mom -
Reflection Connection
should be a daily habit
that changes the day
of your life...
love Gary

DEDICATION

A personal dedication to all my wonderful, life-changing experiences that I have had the opportunity to reflect upon each day. It is purposeful reflection connections that allow us to shape our thoughts, inspire and stretch our feelings, that create responses promoting self-awareness and fulfillment in life.

CONTENTS

ACKNOWLEDGMENTS

To my encouraging wife; Kimberly, who continues to challenge me to be a better person, a more effective writer, and to see the world differently.

To my loving children – Shandee, Brit, Emily, and Cady – may this book serve as a part of my legacy for you to share with your own children, the next generation, and for all those that follow.

To my siblings – Susie and Steve – who's loving support is 'Family Strong' – thank you for being a special part of my continuous journey. To my brother; James – your strong spirit continues to inspire me to keep writing!

To Emily Gasaway, Shandee Rae, Cady Pranke, and Kim LaPorte as they did such wonderful job's in editing and proofreading. You all made this effort exciting and fulfilling!

To all my Friends as they continue to support and inspire me to be my best.

Gary R. Gasaway

Introduction

Do you reflect upon your life?

The answer is yes. We all do. But, do we experience purposeful reflection connections that create better self-awareness promoting enrichment in our lives? The answer unfortunately is few truly experience the essential and wonderful stage of effective reflection – connecting with them.

For most, our reflecting derives from unconscious efforts of unintentional thoughts. Why not create purposeful reflections – ones that you truly connect to? It is purposeful reflection connections that allow us to shape our thoughts, inspire and stretch our feelings, and create responses that promote self-awareness. If this self-awareness is embraced and applied to learning, it leads us to personal growth which produces enrichment in our lives.

The cycle of connecting with our reflections begins with our thoughts and feelings regarding an experience we wish to reflect upon. With thoughts and feelings created, the reflection then moves to an effective response. It is with effectiveness of the response that provides the level of connection you will experience from your reflection.

In short, reflection connection is created intentionally to embrace your thoughts and express your feelings. These thoughts and feelings lead to responding with authority for this creates the foundation of connecting to life experiences. Reflection connection is the most effective way to engage self-awareness that results in enriching your life.

In other words, instead of letting the world create you, you direct the paths of your own world through reflection. With reflection connection, you can discover the real peace and fulfillment you seek in your life.

Reflection connections are all about your inner world of being, which in turn, affects your outer world of doing. This deep, intentional process allows you to make better sense of your present existence and the opportunity to create the world that could be.

True reflection connection is first, learning more about how we respond to our reflection, then taking that learning and applying it for our personal growth. Reflection connections intentionally expand our thoughts, which in turn create powerful feelings. Being intentional in reflection connection is a focus with purpose. This driven purpose is meant to inspire and transform you towards improving your life.

When we think of reflecting upon our lives, many of us will focus on those memories that made unique impacts upon our lives. Unfortunately, not all memories are positive events. Our reflections are a continuous series of good and bad. They are not always filled with joy, but out of sadness as well. It is a reality that there are both successes and failures in life. Many occasions while reflecting upon our life, we focus on our failures. These failures have the potential to bring us down. It is in these times of reflection we can beat ourselves up and make ourselves feel small, or we can learn by them to build ourselves up. Yes, even with failure, we can choose wisdom from this learning while improving in the wake of our mistakes. Mistakes are a vital part of life and we make choices regarding how we approach these mistakes in a positive or negative manner. We alone must choose.

To make a choice and stand firm to build ourselves up even after the worst of circumstances will allow us to grow from any difficult experience. The fact remains, we will reflect upon these difficult times, we just won't focus upon them. Why? Because the potential of negativity closes our mind, not allowing the possibilities of learning, thus improving from these reflective experiences.

Reflection Connections Happen in You

Reflection connections happen in you. Too many times we are focused only on what happens to us. We forget that we alone direct how we think and feel within. Many of us will allow someone or something to influence us in ways that makes us feel embarrassed or have low self-esteem. It is then up to us to dictate what happens within us, not by some outside source. Case in point, there are many that try too hard to understand where they wish they were or where they had hoped to be in life, but where that truth lies is within us.

The fact is, reflection connections promote self-awareness – and self-awareness enables us to see within ourselves more clearly. It is self-awareness that opens the doors to our mind and hearts that bring enrichment into our lives. Reflection connections help us see ourselves for who we really are. A clear view of ourselves is vital for new perspectives regarding where we are to where we desire to go in life.

'Memory Markers' – Written on Your Heart

We all engage in reflecting upon our life and will often go to fond memories that we have experienced. When we connect upon these special times, it's like reliving them all over again.

It is these special times that I refer to as 'memory markers.' It's amazing to me that we can remember an event that may have occurred years before. Like the writings on stone, these memories on your heart are permanent.

When we seek these special moments, we can find them through reflection. These are impressionable moments that we connect to and take to heart – a trip or vacation that you truly loved every minute of, unforgettable people, or special events in our life. These are the ones that are written on our heart. It is moments such as these that take us to the past to reflect upon them whenever we need or desire – today, tomorrow, anytime – now that's special.

Learning from Our Mistakes

We can simply choose to continue to produce the same mistakes or make choices to embrace the learning that reflection connection allows us to experience. When we reflect deeply upon mistakes that occurred from the past, we can also develop steps to learn from them.

In the real world, life is not always surrounded by successes. The truth is, life also includes our mistakes, or how I like to think of them as learning opportunities. The wonderful experience of reflection connections is that they help us to improve our self-awareness in learning more about ourselves to make better decisions moving forward in life.

Learning from our mistakes is wonderful, but it means little if we don't know how to turn the lessons into benefits – it is the learning and lesson application regarding reflection connections that are the foundation to experiencing the benefits from our mishaps.

Pausing and thinking about what we could have done differently to change the actions of our past to successes are the benefits we are searching for when reflecting upon them. In truth, mistakes are just opportunities for learning something new about ourselves to enhance our lives.

Embracing Learning from Our Past

The past is filled with many opportunities to learn. Don't just focus on mistakes, but all experiences from the past. Reflection connection regarding our past experiences is the key to better understanding ourselves. Unfortunately, many don't take the valuable time to pause and reflect each day. The consequences of not taking this beneficial time to reflect, results in limiting the uncovering our past and therefore less opportunity to connect with those experiences regarding the valuable lessons that lie within them.

It is by choice that we initiate reflection connections regarding our lives. If we realize the importance of truly embracing who we are and experiencing reflection connections each day, we then can move closer to fulfillment in life.

Chapter One

'Jogging Your Memory'

This book is designed to create a sense of 'jogging your memory'. This will provide a foundation for you to begin your own journey of reflecting upon experiences and making connections to all those 'memory markers' that are stored within you. Memory markers are those experiences that are most important in your life. These experiences are both very positive and passionate, while others can bring hurt and sorrow.

The concept and motivation behind this book derived from my 'reflecting upon reflections' – all of us have something in common – we all reflect. We are not always aware when we do it, but all of us reflect. It is from focusing on our self-awareness while reflecting that connecting to them begins to take shape.

The focus of this book is to be purposeful. Having purposeful reflections of thoughts, feelings, and responses – then connecting to the intended learning of each reflection. This will promote personal growth which is the goal of all reflection connections.

Another way to consider these purposeful efforts is a deep self-awareness of 'thinking about what you want to think about'. With this self-awareness, you get to choose what you want to reflect upon. With this freedom to choose our reflections is only for us to decide – it's purposeful.

It's purposeful because you go beyond just thinking and feeling regarding your experiences, to connecting and responding with the question: What must I do? You ask this question first because it is linked to a foundational action you reflect upon. That action is part of the connection you make with the reflection. Now, also understand that you have choices as to how you respond – the reflection can simply go back into your memory banks, or you can intentionally connect to them and take necessary actions to promote better self-awareness from the experience.

It is with purposeful and actionable responses you take after your reflections that the connection of growth begins to take shape. It's truly going beyond your thoughts and feelings to engaging in the necessary responses that create the foundation of learning based upon your reflections.

For the intentions of this book; as you read and review the reflection connection examples I share, you are simply responding to the reflection. In fact, you can write notes in the margins next to the ideas I share with you regarding your own thoughts, feelings, and responses. Remember, this is your book. You will naturally want to respond to each example with your own thoughts and feelings regarding the reflective subject I have provided. Don't hold back. This is part of the reflection connection process. Responding is the first step to connecting with your reflection.

Intentional responses start with questions. Again, with our reflections thoughts and feelings move to a responsive question of – What must I do? This question should be instinctive because it is the foundation of responding with authority that is followed by the next question – What can I learn from this reflective experience?

This question then should be followed by – What is the opportunity of growth I can apply from this reflective experience? Because these questions require actions, your answers will then lead you to effective reflection connections.

Just the pure opportunity to reflect upon the previous or present day and then rediscover and connect to the events that 'what was' or 'what is' continues to amaze me. This same opportunity is a gift. Gifts like this are great but it's unfortunate that not all reflections are pleasant experiences. The truth is, even the unpleasant events in life are vital for us to learn and promote a deeper understanding of who we are. It will be this deeper understanding of ourselves that will allow us to move closer to reaching our fulfillment in life.

If you take the approach that all events in life are not by accident – that everyone and everything that you reflect upon has a reason, you will then begin to experience every event – no matter how difficult or challenging – as an opportunity for connection resulting in the enrichment of your life.

Reflections can be instantaneous, right after an event, or they can be yesterday, a week, a year, or even from experiences decades ago. The wonderful thing about reflections is they are always stored in our minds and in our hearts to be released if we choose to reflect upon them. In addition, reflections that are important to us can be repeated, especially those that had a deep impact on us.

Reflection connections can inspire you to change who you are and who you desire to be. It is my hope that by reading and embracing these collections of reflection connections that the journey in which you take will encourage you to pause and think upon pursuing and connecting with your own 'memory markers'.

Chapter Two

Seven Areas of Reflection Connection

As there are many areas of reflection connection, I have chosen only seven common areas of reflection that I believe are the same focus for most individuals in creating a connection. Here are those seven areas:

1. Reflections Regarding Thoughts

As I reflect, how can I better focus upon my thoughts today?

All reflections start with our thoughts. What we think becomes what we feel – and what we feel then becomes the responses we produce regarding connecting with our reflections.

When we think and reflect upon our lives, it's an opportunity to remember and appreciate our positive experiences. This reflective time is also our opportunity to hopefully learn from any undesirable concerns that may have created adversities in our past. Whether the reflection experience is positive or negative, there are always opportunities to think differently, leading us to new perspectives to better embrace and enhance our lives.

We also must strive to think for ourselves; therefore, we choose to oversee our individual direction and what we desire to be in life. We possess the freedom to become what we think – it is an attitude, and with the right attitude, anything is possible.

2. Reflections Regarding Points of View

As I reflect, how can I learn from my points of view regarding past and present experiences?

The cycle of reflection connection begins with our thoughts. Next is feelings, or how we view our experiences. It's vital to focus upon our viewpoints while reflecting. Our individual viewpoints are initiated by choice – and it is this choice that starts on the inside and is seen in our character on the outside.

Our point of view is the foundation of anything in life – with people, our careers, and the choices we make in life. For instance, a person with a positive view of the world has a much better chance against negative reflections and the unpleasant or unfortunate experiences that have transpired in their life.

3. Reflections Regarding People Connections

As I reflect, what relationships stand out the most in my past and present?

Reflections regarding people connections can bring joy and happiness, and in some cases – sadness and despair. People connections can be acquaintances, close friends, lovers, or family – somehow you are connected to all of them.

There are positive and negative people connections in our lives. We have a choice to not dwell on the past negative people connections, but rather reflect upon what we learned from them; thus, resulting in the enhancement of our overall joy and happiness in life. That's what a simple life should represent – happiness. One that primarily focuses upon more joy and happiness in your life and not the people who brought you down or caused pain in your life.

4. Reflections Taken to Heart

As I reflect, which of my life experiences are my most memorable that were taken to heart?

Following reflections regarding people connections are those relationships of love and compassion. These reflection connections are those we hold closest to our hearts. Reflections taken to heart are often underestimated. The key is permitting your heart to be your guide regarding all reflections. In other words, allow your heart to do the thinking.

With the heart, there are emotions – feelings that create the foundation to connecting and learning more about yourself and the passionate experiences regarding loving relationships with others on your journey called life.

5. Reflections Regarding Moments in Time

With time so precious, how can I better use it to be most effective while reflecting upon my life?

Reflection connections regarding moments in time provides us with unique perspectives. Some moments are longer than others; but all moments present us with a variety of experiences.

Time is precious. Think about life overall – it's all revolved around time. And because everything is revolved around time, we do our best to try to control how we use our time. Unfortunately, time is not for us to direct, it keeps moving forward regardless of our demands. In other words, observe any clock. The seconds, minutes, and hours continue ticking forward no matter how you may feel about the time in your life.

We all want more time, but most of us don't manage it well and our time gets away from us. We all make excuses for seemingly not having enough of time but then how many of us make excuses for not using it effectively? Bottom line, we all need to improve the use of our time.

6. Reflections Regarding Lessons Learned

As I reflect, what are my most memorable lessons thus far in life?

Reflection connections regarding life's lessons leads us to self-improvements. Lessons are learned by past experiences that we have reflected upon.

Life is meant to be a continuous journey of learning. It is learning that leads us to knowledge and this wisdom moves us to self-improvement. Lessons are designed to provide us with unique, and sometimes undesirable experiences, to advance us towards our full potential in life. Truly it is our lessons that are presented to us that ultimately lead us to self-improvements and greater joy in life.

7. Reflections Regarding Self-Improvements

As I reflect, where have I improved most from my life experiences?

It is from our lessons in life that result in the foundation of self-improvement and personal growth. True personal improvement is continuous. The key to continuous improvement is to stay hungry. To stay hungry, we must focus our attention upon the reflecting of each experience as it unfolds. Reflecting in this way will always bring about lessons that are meant for us to improve ourselves and our lives.

All these experiences affect our attitude, character, passion and purpose which are all a part of enhancing and improving our life. When we take the time to reflect upon our lives regarding both the joys and disappointments, we then have the unique opportunity to embrace learning more about ourselves. When we emerge from reflecting upon our daily experiences, we then discover a new appreciation of who we are and the life we lead.

Chapter Three

Prepare, Release, Reflect and Connect

To get the most out of connecting to our reflections, we must take the time to prepare, release, then reflect upon our experiences for connection to take shape. These steps must be intentional in thoughts, feelings, and responses. These vital steps will inspire you to reach deep within, to truly reflect upon your past and present experiences. By going deep within, you can connect to reflective experiences with not just any response, but life-changing intentions that can create effective reflection connections.

Reflections allow us to shape our thoughts, inspire and stretch our feelings, and then apply the understanding of our life's lessons to make the reflection connection possible.

Prepare

First, find a quiet place to sit and close your eyes to be completely centered. Your location should have minimal distractions. Preparing requires relaxation, which also means no movement.

Second, focus on your breath. Take several slow inhalations, exhaling slowly and completely.

Third, pause deeply for the reflections to enter your heart and soul. When we take our thoughts and feelings to heart, there may be a mixture of both joy and sadness. It's only a fact of life that we all experience positive and negative events.

Everyone loves when something positive happens in their life, but having a negative situation occur is not the end of the world. Why? Because we can find positive benefits even in the worst of times. One great benefit is the lessons we learn. It is usually from these negative experiences that we connect with life lessons and have opportunities for deeper understanding of our self-awareness which affects personal growth.

Release

Now open your eyes, as well as your mind, and especially your heart. With your mind, thoughts are presented. Through your heart, feelings are released. It is the combination of these thoughts and feelings that produce the responses from our reflections. It is from these intentional responses that we begin connection with our reflections.

The key is to free yourself from distractions so that you are open to all circumstances that enter your mind and heart – both the positive and negative.

This is an opportune time to ask yourself questions first; simply respond to the reflection, then, determine what actions you could take regarding the reflection.

Have No Fear Asking Questions

Before asking possible life-changing questions, you must release any fears you may have regarding the important questions that must be asked of yourself.

Do not allow fear to suppress your thoughts. Fear can bring both denial and avoidance. With denial and avoidance, they can be a way of self-protection – especially when reflecting upon difficult times regarding the past.

Do not judge, just be honest with yourself. It is when you don't judge yourself that any pre-determined fear can be released. Remember we cannot change the past, but we can affect a more positive view of the future by reflecting upon our past. It is essential to challenge ourselves to release any fears and move through the discomfort long enough to begin the awareness and healing process.

The Power of Questions

With freedom from any fears that you may have had in asking yourself deep, personal questions, now release the power of questions that will create the answers you are searching for in your life. Why would you focus upon questions when what you really crave are the answers? It's quite simple. Answers come from questions, and the quality of the answer is directly determined by the quality of the question. So, ask the wrong question, get the wrong answer.

Then it makes sense to ask the right question, get the right answer. Not really. There are many ways to ask the right question, but most of the time, we ask easy, quick fix questions to get to an effortless, right answer. Think bigger – now ask the most powerful question possible, and your answer can be life altering. I think you get the point.

The Power of Questions Regarding this Book

At the beginning of each chapter, I will provide an overall initial question for an inspiring focus of the chapter you are reading. In addition, there will be two questions at the end of each chapters' introduction to put special emphasis upon the specific topic you are reading regarding the collection of [5] reflection connections for that chapter.

Those are:

1. What can I learn from these reflective experiences?
2. What is the opportunity of growth I can apply from these reflective experiences?

Note that these two questions leave nothing to chance. By using the expressions of 'What can I ...' and 'What is the opportunity...' both represent affirming and action-oriented phrases that will result in creating connection and positive outcomes. Positive outcomes are only possible by fully 'experiencing the experience'. It is through experiencing the experience, or action-oriented responses, that true reflection connection begins.

Reflect and Connect

Think about what you want to think about. Be patient. Reflections take time developing into powerful connections with your past, present, and future. The goal in reflection connection is to initiate new perspectives to embrace your life; thus, enriching it towards fulfillment.

Reflection connection goes beyond thoughts and feelings to embrace who you are and where you want to go in life. Being successful in embracing your life will require daily discipline and developing a habit.

Daily Reflection Connection Requires Discipline

Be disciplined to connect. To create discipline, you must reflect daily and be intentional regarding effective reflection connections – continually embracing the intended learning to enrich your life. It is this enrichment that leads to fulfillment.

It's true that the reflections of yesterday motivates your discipline today, and discipline each day maximizes your decisions you made yesterday. That is a powerful statement requiring great efforts and focus – or intentions. Being intentionally disciplined will result in successful reflection connection.

Being disciplined while reflecting upon your life each day matters if you are to live a life that moves you closer to fulfillment. As reflecting requires deep thoughts and focus, it will be the intentional responses that initiate action steps for you to have an effective connection. The results of an effective reflection connection will help in creating personal growth and the fulfillment you seek.

The key to this type of discipline is to always find ways to learn from both positive and negative circumstances. Keep in mind, there are always opportunities to learn more about yourself and the world around you.

Daily Reflection Connection Creates Intentional Habit

Being disciplined is the foundation to creating intentional habits. If you want to improve reflecting upon your life, it must be an intentional habit. An intentional habit is what you do continually, not occasionally. Inspiration and motivation will get you going to initiate reflection connection, but it is only the intentional habit that is developed and practiced where reflection connections can help change your life. With this intentional habit practiced each day, there is no thinking involved, it just happens automatically. This is so powerful that put another way, reflection connections will not change your life in a day but reflecting and connecting with each experience as they unfold will change your days for life.

Are There Barriers to Reflection Connection?

Yes. The biggest barrier to reflecting each day is time. Life comes at us at an alarming speed and if we don't recognize it, life will literally pass us by. With family and career commitments, plus the overall daily pressures of life, we tend to put past, and even present experiences into our 'memory banks'.

Unfortunately, we then wait until later in life when we believe we have the necessary time to rediscover these memories. Sadly, reflecting upon our lives waits until that time. And that time is usually in our twilight years.

Why Wait When You Can Start Today?

We get so consumed with life that we become disconnected with ourselves. Sometimes we are so concerned with finding ways to fill every minute of every day that we tend to forget to just pause, think, and reflect. It's time to reconnect and re-center with yourself. Embark on a new mission – one that makes reflection connections a vital part of everyday life.

Chapter Four

Let's Begin Our Journey

So, let's begin our reflection connection journey. I have designed this book to not only inspire you to reflect daily, but to initiate your thought process. The examples regarding the collection of [5] reflection connections in each chapter will begin with a subject matter title and brief introduction.

This structure will provide focus to inspire your own thoughts, feelings, and responses. These word-association titles are used to emphasize the reflection connection subject being used in each example so that you go beyond thinking about the readings to creating powerful impressions behind the written words.

After this brief subject introduction, I share thoughts and feelings that are developed from the subject. It is our thoughts that lead us to reflecting upon similar events that have occurred in the past. Once we think about the specifics of past events, it is our feelings connected to those events that arrive. These feelings become the foundation to how we want to respond to the reflection.

It is then that I will follow each reflection of thoughts and feelings with a purposeful response to help promote your own individual attachment with each reflection connection to inspire you to reflect upon your own experiences in these specific areas. In other words, the design of these thoughts, feelings, and responses are brief to provide the foundation for you to expand upon them.

In the development of this book, the intentions are for you to briefly look inward to encourage and inspire you to expand upon your thoughts, feelings, and the responses that are not only placed in the book, but your own reaction to the reflection connections. Why? Simply for you to be inspired to develop your own individual reflection connections. This intended structure will ultimately lead you to your own learning and growing opportunities as you reflect upon your life experiences.

This book contains a collection of different reflection connections in specific areas of reflective thoughts, points of view, people connections, taken to heart, moments in time, lessons learned, and self-improvement. Using these specific areas, my hope is to inspire you to create personal reflection connections of your own.

As I am sure it is the same for most of you, I have literally thousands of reflection connections to select upon. For purposes of this book, I only chose a collection of [5] reflection connections in each area of my most memorable ones.

At the end of each chapters' introduction, I will prompt you with the two questions to not only inspire you, but for you to truly think about what actions you would take in connecting regarding the importance of deep reflection.
Those questions again are:

1. What can I learn from these reflective experiences?
2. What is the opportunity of growth I can apply from these reflective experiences?

By taking appropriate actions, you will better understand how important it is to learn and grow from 'experiencing the experience' of each reflection connection you read.

Designing This Book and Reality

While designing this book, the focus is to keep the reader involved by creating powerful and helpful information while in reflection connection. In keeping the information practical, yet simple, I also know the reality of time. When someone mentions that 'It will take some time' to do something, many times our immediate response is 'How can I fit one more thing into my life?' Knowing and understanding this reality, I designed each reflection connection example to be clear, concise, and to the point. The focus is to get you to reflect each day. To make each reflection connection brief, yet effective, is to inspire you to take at least 20 minutes daily to create your own reflection connections and at the same time, to manage each moment. The possibilities are endless, and you can truly have quality reflection connections in just 20 minutes daily.

The reflection connections shared in this book are meant to inspire the foundation to your own connection to each reflection. The overall objective of reflection connections is to be inspired in discovering new learning from each reflective experience so that you can apply it to your life. By applying these lessons, they will bring enrichment and fulfillment into your life.

Once you have read each reflection connection example, take the necessary time to think upon your own experiences regarding the subject. You might consider reviewing the chapters and selecting just one reflection connection daily. By taking just 20 minutes of reflecting each day, you can change the days of your life.

Now, discover the powerful possibilities of enriching your life by embracing reflection connections.

Chapter Five

Reflective Thoughts

As I reflect, how can I better focus upon my thoughts today?

This chapter contains a collection of [5] reflection connections regarding thoughts – or – as I like to refer to them as 'thinking about what you're thinking about'. Everything starts with a thought. A true connection to your thoughts is a conscience effort to focus on these thoughts, while at the same time, exposing feelings of emotional connections of current and past situations. All reflections start with our thoughts. Our thoughts begin the cycle of a reflection connection. What we think, becomes what we feel – and what we feel, then become the actions we could take regarding the reflection we are experiencing. Actions begin with our instinctive responses to the reflections. Once the actions are initiated, the connections begin to take shape.

When we take the necessary time to pause, think, and then reflect, we are directing where and what we will be in life, mastering our fate – possessing the freedom to become what we think. Reflection connection is a focus that we choose to think about. What we think leads to an attitude, and with the right attitude, anything is possible. Think about your own attitude. Where has it led you in life?

A reflection can be short or long term, simple or complicated, but it is our attitude that carries us throughout each reflection connection we experience.

When we reflect, this is the time that we take to pause and process our thinking. It is this thinking time that allows us to gain perspective upon both successes and failures so that we can find the lessons within them and more importantly – making connections to them. This process of connecting to your reflections then opens to deeper self-awareness which then leads to creating responses, or actions to apply personal growth.

As you read this chapter, review each reflection connection and think about those events and situations that will initiate and inspire your own individual reflections that are related to what you read in the examples I have shared. Again, the focus is regarding your thoughts. To assist you, here are two questions to keep in mind as you read each reflection connection – (I suggest writing your own thoughts, feelings, and responses as they resonate with you in the margins. This is your book, your own individual reflection connections, and you should use this book not only as a reference, but as a workbook of sorts)

1. What can I learn from these reflective experiences?
2. What is the opportunity of growth that I can apply from these reflective experiences?

Now, enjoy the journey of reflection connections …

[1] What You Think

We start with what you think because what we think defines who we are. Our thoughts and how we use them determines what we say and do each day. So, what we think becomes critical when we begin our reflection connections. Our thoughts, and what we ponder, create how we feel about ourselves and the world around us. Thinking, then feeling, becomes the foundation to responding to our reflections.

Thoughts and Feelings

Have you ever reflected upon the phrase that goes something like ... *it is all about who we say we are?* This one phrase starts with what we think. It is because what we think defines who we truly are. The way in which we reflect and what we think are completely under our direction. Where our mind goes, we follow – we become what we think. What we think and reflect upon determines our day and how we live it.

As you reflect, ask yourself ... Who directs my mind? The answer is you. Do not let the outside world direct it – do not allow others to influence you regarding the way in which you want to think about yourself.

Reflections upon our thoughts become feelings, and these feelings determine how we act. In reflection we can change how we think and, in turn change our feelings and thus, altering our actions. In other words, we direct our thoughts, feelings, and actions as they unfold regarding each experience. People believe events cause what we feel. These feelings are a natural response – automatic – then you choose what to do with them.

But it is first what we think, then it is telling ourselves about these events that initiates how we will respond. It is from both our thoughts and feelings that are vital tools when reflecting upon life's experiences.

Response

We can direct our own reflections and what we think – not from some outside source. Unfortunately, there are those who are conditioned to think narrow-minded thoughts and are controlled by or strongly influenced to think like others they spend most of their time with. This is no way to live life. What and how we think determines how we live our lives. It is our responsibility to take charge of our own life.

It is all within our control of what we reflect upon and how we think. In other words, this control is our corner of freedom. Effective thinking is about responding with ability and that kind of ability is an awesome force when used passionately to connect with our reflections.

It is vital to be in control of your thoughts as you begin your reflections. With this control, it will determine where you go with your feelings regarding your reflection, and therefore establish how you will respond. With control of your thoughts it also means that you can experience positive thoughts while reflecting; thus, resulting in positive outcomes to your connections.

[2] The Way You Think

Reflection connection begins with what we think, then moves to the way in which we think. The way in which we think makes an important difference in how we approach each reflection connection.

After we decide what we think, next is then how we approach our thoughts. Just as what we think about has its own importance, it is the way in which we think that creates our viewpoints throughout the day. When we begin to reflect, we establish how we see things – our perspective or viewpoint. These viewpoints then become the way in which we think.

Thoughts and Feelings

Reflecting and living life internally is your responsibility. It starts with what you think. Again, it's important to understand – first what you think, then secondly is the way in which you think.

Taking responsibility in living happy and effectively, is a choice we all make or don't. The emotions of being happy are feelings that are created by the way in which we think. The ability to think and reflect in a positive manner, then respond with control and take charge of our life lies within us. A productive life is about taking responsibility for our thoughts, feelings, and actions.

Our life's journey is full of events; good and bad. We have no control over most events, but we do have control over the way we think and how we respond to all events through our reflection connections.

Response

A response after any reflection is initiated from the foundation created by our thoughts. Understand that we cannot always choose what happens to us; but we can always choose what happens within us. In other words, some things in life are beyond our control and it is up to us as to how we want to respond within.

Those that stay thinking that their life is beyond control are only victims of their own reality. Then there are those that take responsibility for their lives and create a way of thinking that embraces positive choices. Those that think in this way have a much better chance to also create a positive attitude towards their circumstances. How we think and respond is completely under our own guidance. Our attitude and how we respond is the difference. It comes down to the way we think.

The way in which we think and reflect starts with our viewpoint. It consists of happy or sad, positive or negative – we choose. It is important to understand that we alone choose our viewpoints – not from some outside source. It comes from within. It's our choice to 'think about what we want to think about.' The opportunity to connect becomes possible after we give much thought to our choices of reflections regarding what and the way in which we think.

[3] Your Worth

What we think of ourselves matters. If we allow negative reflections of ourselves to enter our thoughts, it affects our self-worth. When we don't value ourselves, it is our self-worth that is in jeopardy.

Remember it all starts with what we think of ourselves, which then determines how we feel about ourselves. If it is true that our self-worth begins with what we think, we also have a choice to change what we think if it is less than our current thoughts of ourselves. Changing what we think of ourselves from feeling low self-esteem to positive self-worth is the difference maker. We become the difference maker. We get to choose our worth. That is our corner of freedom.

Thoughts and Feelings

Reflection connections allow us to think deeply upon who we truly are. When reflecting, our self-worth is based on what we think. If we believe we are valued, we will feel valued.

On the other hand, if we think and reflect upon having low self-esteem, then we will feel less of ourselves. The key is in what we think. Just like asking ourselves 'who we are', it is our own self-worth that provides us with how much we value ourselves.

Unfortunately, our self-worth is often based on what we believe the people in our lives think of us. It is when we allow these same people to say or do something directed at us that brings us heartache and pain affecting our self-esteem. It is during these times that our worth can be at its lowest. It is through deep reflection connection that we can change this kind of thinking about ourselves.

Response

Believing in ourselves starts with positive reflective thoughts – passionate thoughts expressed and demonstrated by our actions. These actions are the results of being fully connected to our reflections.

The challenge exists when we allow others to judge us. If we continue to receive our self-worth from those who are critical of us, the effect then is to think and feel less valuable as we reflect over time. The key is to not accept these judgements. It's about believing in ourselves along with our positive attributes that we possess. When we have positive self-worth – the possibilities are endless.

To believe in ourselves is to have an abundance of self-confidence as we reflect. It is this kind of confidence that can go a long way towards connecting and finding the best in ourselves.

Again, all reflections start with what we think. The key is to focus on thinking positive regarding believing in ourselves. Have the conviction to know that we are truly worthy, accepted, and fully confident that our self-esteem is intact and connected just to ourselves.

[4] Just Thoughts

All reflections are of internal thoughts. It is from external events that create our internal thoughts. Whether you are aware or not, you are always reflecting. Some are just natural thoughts; many others are intentional. It is from the experiences of the external world that in turn, creates our thoughts when we are in reflection connection.

Thoughts and Feelings

Reflection connection is created by our internal thoughts regarding the external world. The outside world has an impact on us regarding what and how we think. For each event that occurs, we reflect upon it and formulate a feeling, and then have some type of response. The response is the foundation to connecting with the reflection.

Without a response from a reflection, it stays in our mind unchanged and remains there until such time we reflect upon it again, if ever. Further connection requires response and is initiated through steps, or actions we take for the outcomes we want most from reflection.

It is through these outcomes that result in affecting or changing our life for the better – and that is accomplished by means of reflection connection.

Unfortunately, unless we are focused emotionally on connecting to outcomes, we will at times, feel as though the situation is out of our control. Yet, our response and how we think and reflect upon any event or situation is completely under our direction. It is within us that thoughts and feelings are stored; but there are times that these thoughts and feelings are affected by outside sources.

When our thoughts and feelings are affected by external events and situations, we are then influenced by them; thus, also affecting our level of reflection connection.

Response

Moment by moment events occur that we experience daily and it is up to each of us individually as to how we respond to them. Any response requires first a thought, secondly reflecting upon it, then a feeling. It is through our reflections that we have direction over how we think and feel.

As a part of responding, we can influence our reflections and change how we feel; then in turn, demonstrating by our actions on the outside. Many times, we blame the outside for how we feel on the inside. It is not easy, but do not let the outside world control what you think – because you can change that. What we think and reflect upon determines what we feel, and we can change what we think.

Taking the necessary time to think and reflect upon each situation, then looking at the positive possibilities of outcomes, will always result in better circumstances and effective reflection connections.

It is through living internally that gives us the freedom to think and reflect upon the thoughts we want – and not be adversely affected by the outside world.

[5] Happy Choices

Reflecting motivates us to choose; but first we must put our thoughts to work. To choose is a choice. Choice is power only you hold within. Release it, and the world is yours. Think about it. We make many choices throughout the day, some just naturally, others with more effort of thought, but they are all choices just the same. This also means that as it relates to our emotions, we can choose to have positive, or happy reflection connections.

Thoughts and Feelings

When we reflect, we also choose what kind of reflections we want to focus upon. Each day begins with choices – how we will feel and how we are going to spend the day. It seems simple that we can choose to start each day positive and happy. If it is indeed so simple, then why is it so difficult for people to be happy? The choice of being happy or negative starts with our thoughts and that begins through reflecting about these thoughts.

Like most things in life, happiness is a choice. It is created by us internally through our thoughts and reflection – not by any kind of outside source. Happiness is within all of us, it just needs to be initiated and released. How do we do this? We simply choose. It all starts with what we think. So, why not have happy, positive thoughts?

These 'happy' thoughts can be best described as an emotional connection of being in a place where you can be positive about life with the healthy mental attitude of being grateful for all things you possess. You create your own happiness by thought, then choice.

Response

The ability to be happy is within all of us. Whether it be a positive thought or feeling, being happy is a choice. But to be truly happy, it is through letting go of negative or unpleasant thoughts and feelings. This can be a difficult task only if we allow these thoughts and feelings to go unaddressed. With reflection we can go deeper into the release of negative thoughts and feelings to get to positives. To begin, a positive attitude is needed. Once you choose this attitude, reflection concerning happiness will be possible.

The key to happiness is to evaluate your thoughts, reflect, and refocus how you spend your time. You start by letting go of any negative distractions. Shake off any self-pity, discouragement, and disappointments of the past and live life with positive passion, enthusiasm, and purpose. Choose to live focusing your reflection connections on possessing happy thoughts, feelings, and actions.

Being happy is one of the strongest emotional connections you can have with yourself. Do not live this or any other day unhappy, negative, or defeated. These disparaging emotions will only bring you down creating more stress and complications into your life. With emotions such as this, reflection connection cannot occur. Change how you think and make the most of each day by reflecting upon happy thoughts – you deserve it.

Lasting Thoughts Regarding 'Thoughts'

Reflection connections all start with our thoughts. Our thoughts direct our choices and attitudes while in reflection. In this chapter, we focused on what we think, the way in which we think, and the emotions that are attached to our thoughts.

It is important to stress that you are in control of your own individual thoughts while reflecting – they are in fact, your corner of freedom. No one can tell you what or how to think. Do not allow others to influence your values and how you think. Remember that we are all unique which also means we all will think differently while taking part in reflection connections.

Chapter Six

Reflective Points of View

As I reflect, how can I learn from my points of view regarding past and present experiences?

I believe it is only natural to have reflection connections regarding points of view following our thoughts. As the previous chapter focused on thoughts, it is what you think that determines your point of view of the reflective experience you choose while in reflection. This chapter contains [5] reflection connections that are focused on our individual viewpoints regarding the world we live in. It is your point of view that is the foundation to the attitude you choose. In other words, it is your point of view that starts with your reflective thoughts before the attitude arrives.

People project on the outside what their point of view is on the inside. Our viewpoints consist of one's thoughts and feelings on something or someone. If everything has something to do with our points of view, then we also have the choice to change it – through reflecting upon them.

Living life is our responsibility, as is our point of view – it is our choice to choose a positive or negative thought. In choosing a point of view, there is no gain in negativity; the alternative is being positive.

If there are reflections of negativity in our minds, we display a sense of unease and despair on the outside. If we allow negativity to enter our mind, many of us would spend more time *listening* to ourselves being negative while in reflection, rather than *talking* to ourselves with positive thoughts and feelings. To have effective reflection connections, the obvious choice is to be positive throughout the experience.

The difference is in our choosing. It seems easy choosing positive, but many have a difficult time in being continuously upbeat. But now think of the alternative, and that is being negative. Allowing negative reflections to influence us only brings more negativity. Why be negative in the first place?

There is another perspective, one of being more positive. To shift into being more positive, we need to take charge of our viewpoints, change our words, respond with ability, manage our feelings, and feed our mind with possibility instead of limitations.

Understand that we cannot always choose what happens to us – but we can always choose what happens within us. It is simply a part of life that some things are beyond our control. None the less, we still have control as to how we respond to even the most difficult situations. It is our viewpoints while reflecting and how we respond to each circumstance that is the difference.

As you read this chapter, review each reflection connection and think about those events and situations that will initiate and inspire your own individual reflections that are related to what you read in the examples I have shared.

Again, the focus is regarding your points of view of past and present experiences. To assist you, here are two questions to keep in mind as you read each reflection connection – (I suggest writing your own thoughts, feelings, and responses as they resonate with you in the margins of this book. This is your book, your own individual reflection connections, and you should use this book not only as a reference, but as a personal journal of sorts)

1. What can I learn from these reflective experiences?
2. What is the opportunity of growth that I can apply from these reflective experiences?

Now let's discover more regarding our reflective points of view.

[1] Happiness

When someone mentions that 'attitude is everything', they are spot-on. Everything we say and do is based on our viewpoints regarding our life and how we live it. When we reflect upon our life, the viewpoints in which we choose will make an impact on each experience we have while in reflection. It is our viewpoints that become our emotional responses to life's events.

And it is these emotional responses that affect our happiness. Being happy is one of the most important emotional attitudes to possess while in reflection. More importantly, it is the viewpoint of our happiness that defines us and how we live each day.

Thoughts and Feelings

Reflection connections regarding our points of view are emotions that we feel within and exhibit on the outside. These points of view are part of our belief system. It is what we believe our viewpoints consist of that are generated primarily by the choices we make.

As these emotions correlate to our happiness; being happy is a viewpoint that we choose. Happiness is one of our more positive emotions. Like most emotions – it starts with what we think. From time to time we reflect upon sadness or despair in our personal or work lives. With this kind of emotion, we feel the overwhelming sense of being lost in the world we live. It is during these times that it is difficult to find happiness in life. Although difficult, happiness is always with us. All we need to do is initiate it. It is with that understanding knowing true happiness comes from within, all we need to do is choose it.

Like most things in life, being happy is a choice. In other words, happiness is created by us internally through reflection and not by an outside source. True happiness is within all of us – it is an emotion of the heart. If we can choose to be happy from the beginning of a reflection, chances are that we will have a positive view regarding the experience as well. Happiness is a positive emotion that transforms into an attitude; but we must create it internally by focusing on being positive during our reflections.

No one person is responsible for our happiness, it is simply a choice we make individually. It is true that others do influence our happiness, but it is entirely up to each of us as individuals to choose to be happy.

Response

Happiness comes from our hearts. So, when we reflect, it is better to focus on what our heart tells us – not by some outside source. In other words, it is not our circumstances that make us happy – happiness comes from within. We have the choice to let the outside world effect our happiness or not – for what we create inside remains constantly within us. In creating happiness, it all starts with how we think. For example, it is a good starting point of being grateful and completely connected to our heart while we reflect. There are so many things in life to be thankful and happy for.

We are the only ones that can direct our own happiness. If it all starts with what we think, then simply think happy. As we reflect; it is our thoughts that begin before our feelings arrive. So, it is vitally important to 'think happy' as it will directly affect our feelings that follow while reflecting regarding an experience.

Happiness is created within and once initiated; it is our choice to sustain it. It's not always easy to always reflect upon good times, but if we focus on being positive throughout our reflections, chances are we will avoid most of the negative and hurtful thoughts that will limit any connections to our reflections.

[2] Fears

Switching from happiness in our reflections, we now turn to having fears about them. It is a reality that life is not always about happiness. We will at times, be drawn to our fears while in reflection.

Then naturally, reflection connections regarding our points of view can bring out the best in us, but also the worst. When reflections turn to difficult occasions in life, our view of the world can change from contentment to being fearful. The emotion of fear can stop us in our tracks.

Like the previous reflection connection regarding happiness, fear is created within. Fear is only a choice that we choose to allow. Because it's a simple choice, we also can change a fear into an opportunity to learn while reflecting.

Thoughts and Feelings

Difficult times of the past and present will sometimes bring about fears we are faced with. Fear is an emotion. Anyone who tells you that they fear nothing, is most likely not being truthful. The fact is, we all live with some level of fear. When we reflect regarding life's regrettable experiences, the difference lies in whether we choose to face these fears. Like all emotions, our fears are stored within.

Many times, we are stopped by fear while reflecting upon an unpleasant experience. If we stop while reflecting, it will also stop any opportunity of connection. We must understand that the fear itself cannot hurt us, but not facing it can result in disappointment. Have you ever faced your fears? And if you did face them down, were the results of exhilaration and confidence that you felt? Most of us would say yes. There is a special feeling of freedom when we face our fears.

Then there are those that choose to not face their fears while reflecting and avoid them altogether. Sadly, there are consequences for choosing to avoid them. Our fears can stop us from truly discovering new perspectives regarding our reflections. The results are limited connections of learning. Limited learning also affects the ability to determine self-improvement areas.

Many do not face their fears and therefore do not move passed them. This is especially true when reflections deal with mistakes we have made in the past. Unfortunately, until these mistakes are dealt with and the fears removed, they will remain unresolved with no possibility of positive reflection connection outcomes.

Response

Whatever the fearful situation, if we take the necessary time to reflect upon it, we know the best way to deal with it is to face it. Regrettably, many know this, but don't move forward because of some type of self-imposed barrier they have within. We must get passed the barriers to face these fears. It is facing these fears that we can identify what they are and then take the necessary steps to resolve them.

When we reflect upon and then take the necessary steps in resolving our fears, we learn from them and gain the satisfaction that we faced the unknown.

Again, the fact is, most of our fears are self-imposed while in reflection – they are a product of what we think. Some fears are real, and we all have experienced a few that have changed our thinking. What about the fears that we have not faced? It is quite simple – just change how you reflect upon them to change how you feel about them.

We all possess the power to rise above our fears and let go of them. This can be accomplished by deep thoughts and reflection upon these fears and why they are uncertainties in the first place. When we let go of our fears, we will then embrace the freedom of the future without doubt or worries.

[3] Gratitude

Gratitude should always be an important viewpoint and a part of our reflection connection practice. It's truly being thankful for all the good in our lives. Each day is a gift and that is why they call it the present. Just simple things such as shelter, food, and clothing are so easily missed if we don't focus our reflecting upon being grateful regarding our life and the way in which we are living it.

Thoughts and Feelings

Reflection connections of happiness and gratitude are viewpoints which can provide daily gifts. To bring awareness to our daily gifts is to focus on all the good we already possess. We all have many good things in our life, we just need to take the time to pause and reflect upon them.

Have you ever taken someone or something for granted? We all have at one time or another. Whether it is someone or something, adverse consequences are the results when they are taken for granted. Before we take something or someone for granted; we think and reflect upon the consequences, then choose. For some, this thinking is not of gratitude, but of selfish reasons. There is much to learn for those that don't possess gratitude.

When we think and reflect upon only ourselves, we lose the true value that gratitude presents. It is when we take the necessary time and effort to reflect upon all experiences that help us understand just how important possessing gratitude is regarding our life.

These life experiences are moment to moment. We must always be aware of each moment, for gratitude opportunities come and go throughout our daily life. Do not miss any opportunity to reflect upon being grateful for all the good that happens to and within you.

Response

Having perspective regarding the way in which we live our life is reflecting upon our past and present, and even upon thoughts of our future. Gratitude is also a point of view. When we create new perspectives while reflecting, it also provides the opportunity to see our lives differently and be grateful for what we have in our lives. Reflection connections of being grateful are a great way to start the day. Living a life with gratitude goes a long way of being thankful for all things. Have you ever made a list of all the things to be grateful for? It may also not be the 'things' you're thinking about.

There are always things in life to be grateful for – it is not money, the house we own, or the cars we drive – it is; however, about the people in our life, our health, and our happiness. These things are most important in our lives and we should be grateful for each one of them.

Reflecting upon gratitude each day for the opportunity to truly live our life – by enjoying it, embracing it, and living life to its fullest, are the keys to being happy. Happiness in life comes from possessing and embracing gratitude. Make it a daily practice to reflect upon at least one good thing you have in your life.

[4] Being Negative

In a previous reflection connection, it related to 'happy choices' and the self-imposed barriers of being negative that we create; thus, stopping us from making effective and positive choices in our lives. When it comes to making choices, we also create choices of how we want to think. It is when we generate negative thoughts that can lead us to incomplete reflection connections.

As soon as the negative thoughts are created, there are barriers already put before us. These negative barriers come to us as unaddressed viewpoints from the past that somehow reappear as a part of our reflection connections. Unless they are dealt with, they will continue to be unaddressed and affect us in a negative way while reflecting upon our lives.

Thoughts and Feelings

Reflecting upon a negative past can sometimes bring about unaddressed viewpoints that we may have experienced long ago. Unfortunately, most of these negative viewpoints are only addressed when they affect us years later.

44

It is a fact of life – negativity is all around us. If we let it, negativity will affect us while we reflect. Having a negative attitude is a choice. Like positive, a negative attitude begins with what we think, and we can change what and how we think – all by choice.

Response

A good example of how negative viewpoints can affect us is through relationships with the people in our lives. Many of our reflection connections are regarding our personal relationships. Our relationships consist of friends, family, partners, work peers, and acquaintances. These relationships have a mixture of beneficial and unfortunately, some unhealthy people connections.

It's also a fact that some of our relationships involve negative people that continue to influence us. We all encounter people in our personal or professional life that for whatever reason, have negative points of view regarding the life they lead. We all have known people whom are just unhappy – negative regarding their life.

At times, we are that person. If we do not attend to this unaddressed negativity, it will affect us and all the people connections we have in our life. Dealing with our own negative viewpoints is never a pleasant task, but it is one that must be addressed for a healthier lifestyle. The wonderful thing about it is, if we start now, the change will be positive and immediate. This change must start with what we think, and what we think while in reflection must be focused on positive thoughts. We can stay positive throughout our reflections if we do not allow ourselves to be influenced by the negative. It is simply a choice we make.

Then there are those that choose to be negative. It is amazing that there are people who choose to have a life of negativity – no sense of gratitude towards anything or anyone.

Unfortunately, there are times that we may go to the 'dark side' of our life while reflecting. This is only natural, but we do not have to stay focused on these 'dark times', we just need to learn by them. To live life with a positive view of the world is the only way to happiness – you choose. It is important to understand that no one can make us unhappy, we have the power to choose to be positive and happy. Do not let other people or your circumstances change how you live your life. Reflect upon the good and you will have a better chance of creating a more positive life.

[5] Upbeat

Moving from negative to upbeat regarding our reflection connections can seem difficult, but truly it's only a choice we make. I believe that given a choice between positive and negative reflections, most would choose the upbeat experiences. Positive or negative – these are the true emotions from the heart.

Thoughts and Feelings

When we reflect, positive or negative viewpoints are emotions that emerge from the heart. What our heart feels will be in response to emotions that can go from happiness to grief, but it is still a feeling of choice. Those choices; if made consistent over time, expand then into habits that form our character and it is our character that defines us.

Have you ever met a person who seems to always be upbeat and positive no matter the situation? They find a positive attitude even in the worst of circumstances. These people look for the positive in any situation. It is when faced with the most challenging times that these same people remain upbeat. Why is that? It is because they refuse to be negative. They don't allow this self-imposed barrier to stop them from being positive. In fact, they have a bit more positive attitude called enthusiasm. Think of the word upbeat and change it to the emotion of enthusiasm. When you take the negative out of your head, you can replace it with something more positive – enthusiasm.

It's important to understand that you will never have enthusiasm in your reflections unless you steadily put some in. Think in terms that to have enthusiasm, you must practice enthusiasm. Practice it daily while reflecting and it will never fade.

If our focus and discipline is on being upbeat and positive while in reflection, we will most likely respond with those same emotions in any situation we experience. If you want to be upbeat, use enthusiasm within to motivate you. It is simply a choice.

Response

If we could take the necessary time to reflect upon, then respond to all events with a positive point of view, we would have less stress and live a simpler and happier life. Then doesn't it only make sense to just choose to be happy? Unfortunately, the answer for many people is that it is easier to be negative. Unlike being positive, being negative takes no effort.

Being negative has its own power behind its action or behavior. You need to ask yourself if there is any gain in being negative. You must reflect upon what is the underlying gain you embrace regarding staying in or creating negativity in your life. To really be free of negativity, you must understand your deeper need of this behavior. Only then, can you free yourself to choose differently.

It comes down to what we focus our reflections of thoughts and feelings most frequently. If we focus on reflecting negative, our thoughts will shift to sadness, anger, and despair. But if we choose to focus on reflecting upon the positive, the results will be more happiness, fun, and love.

It is true, what we focus upon most expands. At the end of the day, it is still about the choices we make. The choices we make today defines us. Becoming who we are – the choices we make – it is really a simple concept, but difficult at times to implement. Why not give it a try? Start by reflecting upon your life with a positive attitude. Be more positive and upbeat in life and experience the results yourself. Believe me, you will be more likely to embrace happiness and be positive more often. When you do, your reflection connections will be much more enlightening and rewarding.

Let's go further. Choices. As you read these words, whatever time it is – morning, afternoon, or evening – think about all the choices you have made thus far today. Many! Have they all been good choices? Perhaps not, but choices you alone created. We live by our choices. Knowing this, would it not make sense to truly be aware of each choice and the possible consequences that are attached to those choices? The answer is an astounding yes! Now, go throughout the balance of your day being truly connected to each choice you make.

Lasting Thoughts Regarding Points of View

All points of views while in reflection will make an important difference regarding the level of successful connection that is created with each reflection you experience.

It truly matters whether there is a viewpoint of negative or positive while reflecting. A negative viewpoint will result in a negative outcome. Being negative while reflecting will only bring stress and despair. But remember, it is a choice as to the viewpoint you choose. Yet the best point of view to choose is being positive. To be more positive, all you must do is think differently. It's not always easy but thinking differently will create new perspectives. These new perspectives will result in more positive outcomes. Not all outcomes will be positive but even in the worst of circumstances, you can always find something positive and a possible learning opportunity.

It will be important for you to focus on a positive point of view while in reflection. Remember that your viewpoint begins with what you think, and it is your thoughts that are the foundation of each reflection connection. Stay positive.

Chapter Seven

Reflections Regarding People Connections

As you reflect upon your life, what relationships stand out most regarding your past and present?

This chapter focuses on people connections with others – past and present. It was difficult to select just [5] reflection connections with how much of our time is spent connecting to others.

We are defined by our relationships with others – both successes and failures. We experience from positive, rewarding, and productive relationships to negative, hurtful, and damaging ones. Therefore, initiating reflection connection is an important component regarding our relationships to not only improve our successful relationships, but especially to learn and grow from our failed relationships. To improve our relationships, we must reflect upon them.

We all have many unique people connections – both past and present – in our life. With partners or spouses, our children, co-workers, bosses, friends and family. Some are close, others are distant; however, how many are truly healthy, happy, and connected? The true answer lies in how you reflect upon these important people connections. All very unique in the types of relationships we have experienced in each of these categories.

When we purposefully reflect upon our relationships from the past, and even the present, we are attempting to connect to them. We choose the level of connection and how it touches us emotionally. When reflecting and connecting upon others from our past or present, it is not motivated by self–promotion or persuasion, it is stimulated by love and concern for them. When we reflect upon our people connections, they fuel our emotions in moving them immediately from thoughts to intimate feelings regarding these relationships.

The extent of your reflection of another person and the quality of trust and respect in the relationship, depends upon the degree of your genuine concern and love for that person. People connections are vital for success in our personal as well as professional lives.

In fact, these connections and how we reflect upon them regarding our relationships, define us and the way in which we live our lives.

As you read this chapter, review each reflection connection and think about those events and situations that will initiate and inspire your own individual reflections that are related to what you read in the examples I have shared. Again, the focus is regarding your people connections of your past and present life. To assist you, here are two questions to keep in mind as you read each reflection – (write your own thoughts, feelings, and responses as they resonate with you in the margins of this book. This is your book, your own individual reflection connections, and you should use this book not only as a reference, but as a personal journal of sorts)

1. What can I learn from these reflective experiences?
2. What is the opportunity of growth I can apply from these reflective experiences?

Here now, are the [5] reflection connections regarding people connections ...

[1] Everlasting Friendships

People connections are many times integrated into our reflections. Most of us will naturally gravitate towards reflections of long-term, or everlasting relationships from the past. Many of these reflections include those close friendships we have experienced. These are the experiences that never leave us, for they are deep within our hearts. However, these reflection connections are also mixed with the good and bad experiences resulting from these relationships.

Thoughts and Feelings

Everlasting relationship memories are deep, emotional reflection connections. Over the course of our journey called life, we can meet a great number of people during those many years. Some of those people connections are true, very close friends. As we reflect upon these close friends, there are very few that we will have lasting memories, or connections with.

Why is this? Because true close relationships are rare. If you really think and reflect upon your close relationships over your lifetime, you will discover that there are many acquaintances, but very few close friends. These close friends are those that you share your most intimate feelings with; that you respect, trust, and value the most with all your heart.

Friendship is more than a simple relationship; it is one of the most beautiful and intimate people connections to cherish. For *true* friendship comes from the heart; it is the connection to special people we can share our dreams, hopes, struggles, pains, and joys with – it is an everlasting relationship.

Response

How many lasting friendships do you have? The key word to focus on is 'lasting'. The answer will vary, but the one constant will be – we have lots of friends or acquaintances, but only a hand full of true close friends. When we reflect, there will be people connections that stand out – the ones with true connection – those we hold closest to our heart.

Everlasting friendships come in a variety of forms; no two alike, but all equally important. Our life's journey grants us a wealth of friendships; like family, every one of them touches our life in some way. It is a privilege to experience and reflect upon an emotional connection to someone special in our life – past or present. Words cannot express the gratitude felt and the memories formed – with each special relationship. It is these kinds of wonderful relationships that create a purpose for everlasting reflection connections.

[2] Special Touch

Like the previous reflection connection regarding everlasting close friend relationships, creating a special touch within another's heart is one of the most intimate and passionate emotional connections you can experience. These are people connections in your life that leave an impression with you. This impression becomes the special touch you feel in your heart. This special touch, or feeling is so strong that both parties feel this emotional bond.

It seems the most memorable and loving relationships are those that touch our hearts in a special way. It is these special people that leave you thinking and reflecting upon them often.

These moments in time are reflected upon often to bring not only a loving and meaningful emotional touch but create a special feeling within your heart as well.

Thoughts and Feelings

Often in reflection connection, we think about the special people in our lives that touch us. In true passionate and intimate relationships, the touch is mutual. It is mutual because in healthy relationships, a special touch needs to be demonstrated to keep happiness and joy in the relationship by both parties involved. The touch of care and love makes a powerful impact. Note that I state, "needs to be demonstrated" – for a person to feel that special touch, actions need to follow the loving words being spoken.

It is while reflecting upon special people in our lives that begins the emotional touch we feel within. There is no better feeling than a special touch given to us and then provided to another. This special touch takes the form of encouraging and loving words, followed by positive actions. These are the words and actions that come at the right time, the right place, and for the right reasons when they are needed most in life. When we are loved by another and provide it back to the other, there is a special feeling felt by both.

Response

When reflecting, there is no stronger emotion that can come close to how a person feels as when they are touched and connected by another. This special connection is one with often no words spoken, but it is a true connection sensed by both.

A special touch is something you say or do that creates a deep sense of different emotions such as – love, kindness, happiness, and joy. Just simple words of encouragement and acts of kindness can make a profound impact in another's life.

This impact, or touch is the result of deeply reflecting upon the special relationship of both parties involved and is the center piece of keeping the relationship strong and continuously growing.

[3] Partnerships

We have all experienced partnerships in life – some professional, others personal. As we reflect upon our partnerships, we will often think about the successes, but also some of the failures and disappointments that existed along the way. There are many lessons that can be learned from both success and failure as we reflect upon relationships with others; especially in our partnerships.

Having a true connected partnership with others takes effort for all parties involved. This effort is equally divided among those in the relationship, not just one person. It is when we only think of just ourselves, that a partnership is not possible. As we reflect upon our partnerships with others, it is not you or them, it is 'we' that should be the focus.

Thoughts and Feelings

When we reflect upon ourselves and focus only on our own needs and wants, there is no room for partnerships. A true partnership and/or a loving relationship is not built on having it one way – but on creating mutual bonds of trust, respect, and being valued by one another.

Having these three components of trust, respect, and providing value in any relationship is the foundation to an emotional connection with another.

Naturally, there will be times of disagreement, but there is always the opportunity to reach a satisfying compromise for both parties. These opportunities and what they present are great subject matter regarding your reflection connections. It is when we reflect and focus upon our self-awareness that we then discover different perspectives concerning our disagreements with others.

Then there are those that do not reflect upon their disagreements with others. Why? Well, a more common reason is pride. These same people think and feel that they are always right and look at others to take the blame for any disagreements. Do you know, or have you met the type of person who thinks – 'My way or the highway' or 'I am right, I am never wrong'? This type of person is not open and knows everything, pushes their own agenda, and is not willing to listen. Is it not a shame that someone would think and feel this way? It is unfortunate that partnerships such as this will suffer with no learning, growth, nor connection. In most cases, these relationships end in anger, despair and hurtful feelings.

Response

Reflection connection allows us to think differently and create a wide spectrum of diverse perspectives. No one person is ever successful thinking and reflecting only upon themselves – their way is the only way, or they are always right.

A successful people connection is built on the different perspectives of each person involved. In true partnerships, the goal is to find a common ground and ensure both parties' needs are met.

Partnerships are built on the uniqueness of having different perspectives but also coming to an agreement when there is conflict. The key is to be open in all aspects regarding relationships. When there is a choice to be right or to be open – choose to be open. When we choose to be open to all perspectives while in reflection, it provides diverse viewpoints to help us better understand our people connections in a different sense. In addition, it also has the capacity to enlighten us and expand upon our life with new perspectives to grow and enrich us.

People who choose to be open, and learn to work with and not against others, are those that create the best and most effective partnerships. These effective partnerships continually reflect upon and strive in finding alternatives to create common ground and nourish productive relationships that lead to successful partnerships.

[4] Listening

If any of us had to create a list of improvements for ourselves, it would most likely have the quality of listening on it. I believe most of us talk more than listen. Why? Because most of us know what we are already going to say to another, and we just can't wait to get the information out. Why? Because most of us are impatient. The fact is, we just want to hear ourselves speak. In other words, when we talk, we are just repeating what we already know. It is when we truly listen that we may just learn something new.

While in reflection, it is important to focus upon truly listening to our thoughts and feelings. Don't rush the reflection process – it takes time to be effective. Be patient.

When we are patient and focus on our thoughts and feelings, it will be these reflective experiences that will result in better self-awareness. The key is when you listen, you will learn.

Thoughts and Feelings

While in any reflection connection, we first experience our thoughts and then feelings. As they relate to successful people connections, one thing seems to always stand out as a necessary quality – listening. Reflection connection is about better self-awareness for enrichment regarding ourselves and the people in our lives. It is when we take the necessary time to actively listen to others that we learn new ideas and perspectives to enhance our lives.

We must trust, respect, and value ourselves while in reflection. We also must reciprocate these same three things towards those we actively listen to. When we actively listen to the other person, we present ourselves in a manner that shows how patient and respectful we are, thus reflecting back love.

Think and reflect upon the last time you actively listened – open to the other person in the conversation – the reward was mutual understanding and deeper connections. Deeper connections that lead to more joy in your heart and life. Is that not the goal in listening? To create a connection with another, there needs to be shared understanding between the individuals.

It is through our reflection connections that we can focus upon actively listening to our thoughts. If we listen deeply to our thoughts while reflecting upon our relationships, we will appreciate a new understanding for how important these connections are in our lives.

Response

If we listen, truly actively listen, with no interruption and with eye to eye contact, a special connection is formed with the other person that we are in conversation with. In addition, if we focus, reflect, and listen with our heart, it adds a whole new dimension to the reflection connection experience whereas both parties feel and are touched with an emotional bond. The beauty of this bond is that no words need to be spoken. It is knowing that each person has deeply reflected upon the loving care they have for one another.

Imagine if we could have a stronger connection with one another – possible through active listening – it is a choice we make each time we communicate. When we make the choice to actively listen, we accomplish the link to understanding one another. Better listening skills leads to not only more effective understanding, but less stress and disagreement. Active listening focuses on face-to-face, eye-to-eye, heart-to-heart – that is true connection with another. Knowing that active listening is an area of improvement for many, make it a point to reflect upon this valuable skill daily.

[5] Serving

Our reflection connections often are those thoughts of experiences whereas we have served another in some way. Successful people connections are based upon serving others. The beauty of these experiences is when you make the effort to serve another, it often comes back to you. When you do something such as a loving and caring act for another, it is felt deep within not just that person, but you as well.

It is this act of goodness that creates warmth within your heart. Again, the simple act of service becomes the foundation of value felt by the other.

Thoughts and Feelings

Reflecting upon our people connections with others will sometimes lead us as to how we can better serve and support others. There are so many unique and simple ways to serve others. The problem is too many of us reflect upon why we can't. These self-imposed excuses are exposed by examples such as not enough time or thinking it's too much of an effort to do something for another.

Do we think and reflect upon our time commitments? And what about our level of effort needed to assist others? We all do. It all starts by thinking and reflecting upon what amount of time and effort commitments will be needed to fit just one more thing into our day. Now, if you really reflect upon time and efforts needed to help others you can usually find excuses why you can't do something. These are usually self-imposed barriers we place upon ourselves. When it truly comes right down to it, providing support of any type is commendable, not to mention providing a wonderful feeling back to the person you are supporting – it's felt by both people. Serving is making a commitment to another in a loving and caring way.

Sometimes our service to others is planned or it may be at the spur of the moment. Whether this service is planned or not, serving others is worth the time effort it takes. If we deeply reflect and consider the demands placed on us daily, providing service to others becomes a bit of a challenge, but only if we allow it to be.

Today, finding time to participate in the lives of others is sometimes difficult. It all comes down to how we reflect upon providing service or supporting others. Again, while reflecting upon serving, many of us find excuses why we can't serve others. Being too busy is not much of an excuse. The point is, we can all make time and provide effort to serve another if we choose.

Response

Regarding helping, serving, or supporting others, we all reflect upon our efforts of sincerity and times of our guilty conscience regarding why we did or did not serve another in need. All of us are guilty of not helping or serving someone in a time of need; yet we all had the ability to do it. Anyone of us can come up with justifications for why we can't assist another, but we know in our hearts how we truly feel about the situation.

Now, pause and reflect just for a moment, how long does it really take to provide a service to another? The conclusion should be that it is time well spent and worth the effort. Not to mention that this kind service makes a powerful difference to the other person that is possibly in a difficult time of need.

Regarding providing service to others, we must be willing to give when called upon; more importantly, to be proactive and not wait for others to call out for support. To take the initiative and not wait to be asked to help another, is one of the most unselfish acts you can do. In successful relationships, people help each other out because they genuinely love and care for one another. Providing service means value. It is when we demonstrate that we value another that it is felt deep within.

So, start today. Take the time to ask others when you know they need help. Take the initiative to support another. Taking time out of our busy lives is time we can never get back; however, they are the most rewarding times when we give to others.

Lasting Thoughts Regarding People Connections

As we reflect daily, it is our relationships, or people connections that are the subject of many of our reflections. Why our relationships? Well, think about just how important our relationships are to us. It is truly these relationships that we ultimately build our most successful connections with.

It is not things, but people in our lives that make the true difference in how we live and define our lives. These bonds are so strong that we take them on our life's journey – these special people become a part of us, as we are a part of them. It is this emotional connection that creates the grounding that we search for in life. Imagine living a life without relationships. Most of us would be lost without those special people that support and love us. It is these special people connections that help us reach our accomplishments in life.

As we take different paths in life, we also meet many people along the way. Many of which we create lasting relationships with, and others will be short-lived because of the type of connection we had with them. When we reflect upon our lives, both good and bad relationships will surface. It will be the good, healthy people connections that will create happiness and joy in our hearts as we fondly reflect upon these experiences.

Chapter Eight

Reflections Taken to Heart

As I reflect, which of my life experiences are my most memorable that were taken to heart?

As we just reflected upon our people connections, it is those relationships that we hold close to our hearts. In these next [5] reflection connections regarding the heart are those special memories of love, joy, happiness, and compassion. No doubt these examples will remind you of some special heart-felt moments in time that you still hold close. They are precious to you.

Then there are other memories of broken hearts that will, in time, eventually help to serve us once we reflect upon them. The fact is, it's healthy to reflect upon those experiences that have hurt us, for those difficult experiences will help us learn more about ourselves, resulting in better self-awareness and personal enhancement.

People who successfully reflect and connect with their hearts and others – also listen with their heart. When we reflect upon and listen with our hearts, we then are more likely to discover our deepest emotions. These emotions, many times go untapped if we don't look for and listen to what they have to say to us. By actively listening to our hearts and what they are telling us, will enhance our reflection connection.

Many of our reflections that are taken to heart consists of connecting to others that bring closeness into our relationships thus; creating a special bond with them. This bond creates a closeness of love and support so intimate that we can listen to one another's heart.

It's only natural that listening and opening our heart may also bring about reflections of hurt and despair from the past. Remember that we will have many loving, heart-felt reflections but we will also have experiences of somewhat hurtful reflections, we just won't focus upon them. By not dwelling on them, we can replace the negative inner voices in our mind with more reflection upon nurturing voices to help build up healthier, more positive thoughts. This process is exactly why we want to reflect. It's good for our soul. The key is to learn valuable lessons by these unfortunate events and to build a stronger heart that is then open for personal enhancement. An open heart as we reflect is the beginning of self-discovery and growth. When we combine both thoughts through our minds and feelings within our hearts, the true connection begins to reveal itself.

As you read this chapter, review each reflection connection and think about those events and situations that will initiate and inspire your own individual reflections that are related to what you read in the examples I have shared. Again, the focus is regarding your life experiences of reflection connections taken to heart. To assist you, here are two questions to keep in mind as you read each reflection – (write your own thoughts, feelings, and responses as they resonate with you in the margins of this book.

This is your book, your own individual reflection connections, and you should use this book not only as a reference, but as a personal journal of sorts)

1. What can I learn from these reflective experiences?
2. What is the opportunity of growth I can apply from these reflective experiences?

Now, take the journey and discover your own reflection connections taken to heart throughout this chapter.

[1] Hope in Your Heart

Anytime we feel as though all may be lost, there is always hope within our heart that we can initiate through our purposeful reflections when we need it most. This deep emotion can make a difference between giving up and moving forward. Hope is a compassionate part of our heart that can keep us optimistic on the inside that in turn, shows us strength on the outside.

Thoughts and Feelings

Whatever challenges we reflect upon, there is no stronger emotion to have on your side than hope. Hope is conceived within our hearts. When all is thought to be lost, we many times think of and reflect upon our negative experiences. With our thoughts already negative, the results then reflect upon a feeling of despair. These hurtful feelings can turn into negative emotions if we allow them to. It is hope that holds the key to whether we overcome these emotional obstacles or quit. Reflecting and connecting upon our emotions of hope provides us strength to keep moving forward regardless of the obstacles put before us.

How do you deal with challenging life situations? For many of us, the answer is to reflect and only barely touch upon what truly needs to be addressed regarding the challenging situation. This level of reflection will not allow for connection that could result in improved self-awareness. By only touching the surface and not addressing these challenging situations, we only then just cope with them. By only coping with the situation, we create an environment based upon the negative consequences it brings.

Simply coping with our challenges involves little more than just slightly thinking and reflecting about them with an inconsequential response. It is in these moments, where hope in our heart can be the difference between overcoming the challenge or quitting.

Response

If we reflect and connect upon the true strengths of hope and what this emotion can provide, we can face whatever obstacle is in front of us. Hope provides us the promise while in reflection that there is always a way, an opening, an opportunity, and quite possibly a positive outcome.

Just the simple act of thinking and reflecting upon the positive opportunities with hope in your heart, will move you from the possibilities of giving up on your reflection connections or staying on course. Not giving up nor giving in regarding your reflection provides confidence that if you have hope, you also have faith. Both emotions work together to help you stay strong in the most difficult of circumstances. Hope is the emotion that provides us the confidence to rise to the challenge. It is then faith that helps us push beyond our limits to a positive outcome. Effective reflection provides strength that our thoughts and feelings connect to hope – a promise to ourselves to never give up under any circumstances.

[2] Broken Heart

As I wrote in the introduction of this chapter, reflection connection brings good and bad experiences to our thoughts and feelings. It is the bad experiences that seem to affect us the most.

Both good and bad experiences affect us in different ways. The good we want to repeat and reflect upon frequently. The bad we would just as soon avoid all together.

When these negative reflections are focused on our relationships with those close to us, there will often be broken hearts left behind. These hearts stay broken until such time we initiate the healing process.

Thoughts and Feelings

When we reflect upon our relationships – past and present – there are times of happiness and there are also times of deep sadness. How easily can our heart be broken over a special relationship, the loss of a loved one, or a friendship? It happens to all of us. In our fragile environment of relationships, breaking hearts are a natural occurrence for many of us, as they will most likely happen on our life's journey.

As we reflect upon relationships, our hearts can become fragile, if we allow the outside to become a part of the inside. The more fragile it is, the more effort is involved to mend it. Mending takes time and extra efforts to move forward from whatever or whomever damaged your heart. There is no timeline for mending, just know that hurt itself is temporary and healing starts when you recognize the hurt and want to take the necessary actions to begin the mending process.

Reflecting upon pain and sorrow from past relationships are especially tough and often it is these sour relationships that leave a torn heart. A torn heart is one that is broken or bruised. Once torn, our heart must find a way to mend. Fortunately, we all have the natural ability of resiliency to help us bounce back.

On the other hand, although we have the ability, there are many that stay in a state of pain and sorrow within thei hearts.

Response

Remember that we have choices as to how we respond whe reflecting upon any given situation or event. This includ reflections taken to heart. No one is immune; at one time another, by a person or event, we all have experienced broken or torn heart. However, we have the choice to mc forward, to mend our heart, and to find connection happiness once again. It is during this mending period are provided with an opportunity to reflect upon our s awareness through even the most difficult times. No ma the circumstances, we can be more self-aware and ap learning and personal growth from any situation.

The best response is to take actions towards mend our hearts. To truly mend the heart, we must keep mo forward no matter what the obstacles. As we reflect, mo these so-called obstacles are ones we put in fron ourselves. Understand that these self-imposed obst; will only delay the mending or healing process.

Once you begin the process of healing, all emotions into more positive sensations. It is only then that our will beat stronger, our smile will return, and we will h spring back in our step. The key is to be open and cre strong connection to your heart while in reflection and with passion and love. The more you open your hear will reap the benefits of endless joy and happiness. Yo it to your heart.

[3] Listen to Your Heart

Previously, we reflected upon active listening regarding our people connections. We also need to listen to our own hearts. Again, one of the most underutilized communication tools is the ability to actively listen. Listening goes beyond just hearing with our ears. When we listen to our heart, it will express passionate emotions for us to use in the opening of our hearts while in reflection.

Thoughts and Feelings

True and purposeful reflection connection motivates us to open our hearts. It all starts with our thoughts to think about listening. It is the combination of deep thoughts and listening to what our heart tells us, that begins the connection with oneself. This is the process that helps us trust our hearts while in reflection and then guides us to make the tough decisions in life. If you can trust nothing else, trust yourself – trust your heart.

All of us can think for ourselves; however, not many of us truly listen to our hearts. We get so caught-up in overanalyzing situations that we forget to take the time to reflect deeply and fully listen to what our heart is saying. It is when we overanalyze anything in life, we can sometimes miss the obvious.

When we reflect, thoughts will take place first. Once the thought has been created, we move to listening to our heart, or feelings. Our heart creates the emotions from the thoughts. It is then our emotions that lead us to actions and it is these actions that create the reflection connection.

Response

Before most of us learn to connect to life's experiences; we relied mostly reflecting upon our thinking abilities to make decisions. We must also recognize that reflection is not just focused upon our thinking abilities, but much is that of our emotions, or feelings. It is at that time that we discover not only do we have deep thoughts, but that these deep thoughts hold an emotional connection to our hearts.

When we reflect upon life's experiences, it is about responding with ability and going beyond our way of thinking and focusing upon passion and the desires of our hearts. By no means am I suggesting using only your heart to make decisions, but simply to listen to it – the heart holds the strong emotions that support us while reflecting that in turn, helps us in making the important decisions of life.

It is when we listen to our heart while reflecting that emotions are focused upon. Thoughts without emotions do not produce results. With no results, your reflection has no connection. To have a complete connection, there must be emotions involved and those sensations originate from listening to your heart.

[4] Caring

When we reflect upon those who are close to us, many feelings are released. Reflections upon caring move from thoughts to feelings quickly. In other words, thoughts are short, but feelings are lengthy and take time to develop from the heart. These feelings are of love, joy, and caring for the special people in our lives. The root of caring is love. It is our reflection connections of loving emotions that come from deep within our hearts.

Thoughts and Feelings

Reflection connection that is focused upon caring creates thoughts of love for another. With love, there is emotion; therefore, we move from our thoughts to emotions immediately. Caring is demonstrated by the loving actions given to another person and felt in the heart. When a person knows we genuinely care, they think differently of us. These caring feelings will continue to build throughout the relationship that earn mutual trust and respect for one another.

The sentiment of care can be shown in many ways. However, if care is shown from the heart, it is the strongest, most passionate gift provided to another. A caring heart demonstrates an emotional connection and the feeling of caring is present within. Unfortunately, many only reflect upon the thoughts of caring for others and don't demonstrate them for a complete connection to take place.

It is when actions are followed through, that people see and feel a sense of being cared for – thus the feeling of being valued. Reflection connection provides us with these thoughts and feelings of others in our life that we genuinely value.

Response

True reflection connection provides thoughts, then feelings; but it is through demonstrating care that others feel valued. Showing you care for another person lets them know that they are important to you. The result is a feeling of being safe and secure. The closeness of this special bond is like no other feeling – for a caring heart is a giving heart. A giving heart is a happy heart.

This feeling of a happy heart brings love back to you and makes your life even more joyful and meaningful. The deepest, emotional touch we can offer is caring. It is best expressed by the support provided during life's struggles. These expressions through acts of love and kindness are displayed by staying emotionally and physically connected – never giving in to the situation or giving up on the person. Never giving in or up are only demonstrated through the actions we take to care for another. The cycle of reflection connection start with thoughts and feelings, but it is only through caring actions after the thoughts and feelings that connection begins.

[5] Giving

From caring, becomes actions of giving. This giving comes from the heart to provide caring for another. With caring being the emotion, then demonstrated with an action of giving, it becomes a wonderful experience. This experience is shared by both the giver and receiver. It is by reflecting upon the act of giving that provides the first step for connecting to the experience.

Thoughts and Feelings

I thought it would be only natural to follow caring with reflecting upon giving. Caring and giving go together. The act of caring starts with passion to live life with a giving heart. A giving heart that focuses on the act of providing something to another would rather give than receive. Memories such as these create reflections of generosity. It is this feeling of generosity that stimulates the positive energy of the reflection.

For when we give from the heart, we provide something that can only be felt deep within another. The value of giving is a great attribute to possess.

Further, to give means to offer without expecting anything in return. When we give from the heart, it is the most unselfish thing we do for another person. One of our rewards is in knowing we have provided something that can be felt deep within by the other. Another reward is that wonderful feeling that glows inside of us. It's an unexplained joy that we only feel with selfless acts of kindness and love. Reflecting upon these special moments will be those taken to heart.

Response

It is a true statement that if you give from the heart based on the wants or needs of another, it will often come back to you. For many of us, it has always been a focus to give rather than to receive. These are great memories to reflect upon.

In giving from the heart, we go deeper into our connection with the other person, we become a part of them – reflection of living within our memories – and in turn, they become a part of us. So, this emotional connection is mutual whereas both parties feel a part of this memory.

Because they are a part of the reflective memory, they are also influenced by the level of connection being created. The fact is, we all can influence others in a way that results in a true connection that builds a stronger relationship. In giving, we exercise the emotion of compassion by opening our heart – thus this same kindheartedness often comes back to us in return at the right time and place when we need it most.

Lasting Thoughts Taken to Heart

Our heart is one of the strongest organ's, but it can be weakened at any moment in time. When we reflect upon our lives, there are many connections that lead us to events and situations that have affected our hearts. These are a lifetime of experiences mixed with joy and happiness and those of sadness and despair.

I believe most of us would rather merely repeat the more positive reflections and just forget or avoid all together the negative experiences. Unfortunately, the reality of life is not filled with only happy times. When we reflect, it is those occasions of sadness and despair that, although hurt or damage our hearts in the beginning, are also the life experiences that make our hearts stronger after the learning takes place.

Chapter Nine

Reflections Regarding Time

With time so precious, how can I better use it to be most effective while reflecting upon my life?

In this chapter, I choose [5] of my most memorable reflection connections regarding time and how to use our time to be most effective in life. Time is precious. Think about life overall – it revolves around time. When I think of time, I know that it is not within my power regarding how much of it I will have while I live out my days. Rather, what I do with my time certainly has influence over how I spend that time each day. We all make excuses for seemingly not having enough time, but then how many excuses do we make for not using it effectively? Case in point, reflecting and connecting each day will take time. To be effective in life and to be more self-aware while in reflection, we must have focused time for comprehensive pausing throughout the day.

The key is taking the necessary time in reflection to pause and truly appreciating the moments of your experiences. When we are more self-aware of time and how we use it, many of us would be surprised as to how many special moments have been missed because we were too busy to notice them as they unfolded. The unfortunate circumstances are that these missed moments may never return.

As you reflect upon your life, how many special moments have you missed because you traded it off for something less important? We all have. We can all improve the effectiveness of our time. It is through reflecting upon our time and how we spend it that will make the difference.

As you read this chapter, review each reflection connection and think about those events and situations that will initiate and inspire your own individual reflections that are related to what you read in the examples I have shared. Again, the focus is regarding your reflection connections and your effectiveness concerning time. To assist you, here are two questions to keep in mind as you read each reflection – (write your own thoughts, feelings, and responses as they resonate with you in the margins of this book. This is your book, your own individual reflection connections, and you should use this book not only as a reference, but as a personal journal of sorts)

1. What can I learn from these reflective experiences?
2. What is the opportunity of growth I can apply from these reflective experiences?

Now, take the journey and discover your own individual reflection connections throughout this chapter.

[1] Time

The saying 'time flies' couldn't be truer. It appears life is always in the fast lane. With technology so advanced these days, it's impossible to keep up with it all. Time will pass you by if you're not spending it wisely. Taking the necessary time to think about reflection connections regarding time will help create purposeful self-awareness and more effectiveness in your life.

Thoughts and Feelings

Do you ever think and reflect upon how much time you have on this journey called life? Most of us have – it is natural to think about it. When we ask ourselves and reflect upon the question of 'How much time do I have?' What are your thoughts? The question is something to ponder, but there is no definitive answer. The truth is – what time we do have to live is not really under our jurisdiction.

Time. How much is considered enough? Most of us will admit that we wish we had more of it. Some of us will say we do not use it as effectively as we could. A few of us will even admit to wasting some time. The fact remains, once time goes by, you cannot get it back.

Time is measured by several components of seconds, minutes, hours, days, months, and years. There are many ways to look at the time we have. When used effectively, time will assist you in managing each moment as it unfolds. It is during reflection connection that you can plan your time and how you spend it. The wonderful idea behind how you spend this time is that it's all under your direction. Imagine not allowing time to control you, but you are managing it the way you want to spend it.

Response

If we understand the true concept of time, we begin to live life differently. We accomplish this with more focus and discipline. The thought of directing not how much time but how it is spent, provides clarity to the concept. In other words, not to waste a second of it! The key is to live each day as if it was your last. If you lived life as if it were your last days, believe me you will live it more effectively.

Time is not for us to decide how much we have of it; but, to decide what to do with the time given to us. No one person really knows how much time they have to live their life. Why not start today and make a conscience effort to be effective and reflect upon the connection with each moment as it unfolds? In fact, each moment unfolds before our eyes. Look around and you will see clocks are everywhere. Clocks reveal each second, minute, and hour of the day. Think of a clock as your personal job aid. As you move throughout the day, the clock records your every move. In this case, use the clock to help you manage each day by reflecting upon how you will spend your time.

[2] Time Effectively

Moving from managing time to effectiveness – reflecting upon the efficiency of how you utilize your time. First, we must understand how we define our time. For instance, what is wasting time to you? It might be waiting at a stop light, in rush-hour traffic, standing in line somewhere, or maybe it's even waiting for the commercials to go by while you're watching television. Whatever that wasted time is to you, do you ever think and reflect upon how you can use your time more effectively?

Thoughts and Feelings

When we engage ourselves into reflection, there needs to be time set aside to think about life. Like time, life is precious – both are interconnected. Can we direct our time and use it the way we want? The answer is yes. We can better manage our time so that we can use it more effectively. So, if this is true, why do we not use time more effectively? The short answer is that we make excuses.

We can all make excuses for why things don't turn out the way we planned. A good plan takes time to implement, so why is it we don't use our time effectively to reflect upon this plan of ours from start to completion? Remember that the time we live our life is not within our control, but the way we spend that time is. The fact remains that you cannot go back in time to do something you had planned to do, but never fulfilled. For so many of us, the time spent thus far has not always been the way we have planned it, nor lived it. The way to improve how we spend our time is to think deeply and reflect upon better choices that can be created so that we are more effective regarding the use of our time.

Response

A good response might be better illustrated by an example I am sure many of us have heard. Most of us are familiar with the story of the man, who upon his deathbed, wished he would have lived his life differently and not focused all his time on his career. Does this describe your current life of spending too much time at the office and not enough time with family and friends? If so, know you have the choice to change how your time is spent. Do not let this become your story.

We can all respond with authority and change our current circumstances. Now is the opportunity to reflect upon the time we have and start living life the way we want it to be. It really is about effectiveness.

Effectiveness is regarding quality of life, not how much, but how that time is spent. We only have the days that lie ahead, and we have the choice to make them extraordinary. We choose the outcome of each day by reflecting upon it, then deciding the way we want to spend the time that has been given to us.

[3] Simple Life

The opposite of a complicated life is a simple one. Why do we make life so complicated? Truly it's only a choice to accept a life such as one that is difficult. As it relates to time, don't let even the simplest things in life pass you by – all moments in time are important and should be experienced, reflected upon, possibly apply some learning, and embrace them as they unfold.

Thoughts and Feelings

Reflecting and connecting upon life is about experiencing major events as well as the simple things that occur on our journeys. Bypassing the simple things in life is somewhat common it seems. Is it because of time or importance? Whether time or importance, our failure seems often to come from reflecting and focusing on the less important things. Are they deemed less important because we don't make the time to truly experience them? The answer is that we need to take the time to enjoy all things in life even the ones that we deem as less important.

You know as well as I, time really does fly – as one-year ends, another begins. As we reflect, one thing that always comes to mind is – where does the time go? In our fast-paced environment, it is difficult at times to make the effort for the little things in life – the simple things. In fact, we even take them for granted on occasion. Taking these simple things for granted is believing we can by-pass even some of life's simplest things for seemingly more important things.

Response

A simple life has many connections. The most important connections are the people in your life. People should never be taken for granted. It is truly the special people in our lives that are most important, and we should be grateful for all their positive influence they have provided us. It is vital that we simply pause and take the necessary time to reflect upon the joy that these special people bring to our life. This is only possible by an ongoing effort of complete self-awareness as we reflect upon those special people that played an important role in our lives.

Take our close relationships for example. These are the ones we truly care for and love. We demonstrate simple and loving actions towards them. These simple things are shown as a smile, listening instead of speaking, or observing instead of doing. It is making the time and effort in lifting someone's spirits to make their day. Although simple to understand, they are the things that matter most in life.

People come and go in our lives. Our journey is comprised of simply time, many people, and several paths to take along the way. They all play a significant part of our journey. Many of these relationships are special to us.

It is when we reflect upon these special relationships that we better understand how important our time is and the significant role and impact these people have made in our life.

[4] In the Past

Reflection connections from the past create the best lessons for the present. As we reflect, we will often go back in time to past events. It is these reflection connections that we can learn from and initiate growth opportunities for the present. Just one reason why it is so important to take the time to pause and reflect upon each day especially regarding past experiences that we have the opportunity to apply valuable learning lessons.

Thoughts and Feelings

The words... 'coulda', 'woulda', and 'shoulda' are considered past thoughts as we reflect upon our lives. The key to successful reflection connections is to leave these thoughts right there – in the past. Why is this? Because there is nothing we can do to change the outcome of past experiences – we can only be more self-aware of them. Think of it in terms of not just reflecting upon your past but learning from the past to experiencing the present differently regarding the possible changes you can make in your life to promote personal growth and greater joy and happiness. If there was an event or unhappy outcome regarding your past, this is an opportunity to create something different. It is you that directs the outcome of any experience. Having this kind of control, provides the fuel to make some positive out of a negative past event.

The past is there only to learn and grow from. Once you have thought and reflected upon it, embrace the feelings regarding an unsuccessful past but then leave it behind. Unfortunately, some of us find ourselves returning to the past only to surrender our feelings to think and reflect upon how we could have changed it. The key is to focus on the present and reflect upon the possibilities and the successes we will encounter each day as they unfold and leave the difficulties of the past – in the past.

Response

We all have beaten ourselves up over bad decisions, mistakes, past issues, and difficult experiences while in reflection. These thoughts and feelings will only discourage you and cease any positive efforts to move you forward in life. The best response is to deeply reflect, forgive yourself and look forward, and leave the past where it belongs – behind you. If we continue to reflect upon and attempt to only live in a difficult past, our lives remain in the past. Because we remain in the past, we then suffer the results that create a feeling of being stagnant and unhappy with our life. Think about all the opportunities and experiences we miss out on if we are stuck upon an unpleasant past.

When our focus is on reflecting and connecting upon moving forward, we develop an ongoing inner feedback of excitement and encouragement for initiating what is yet to be created. This type of forward thinking allows us to be optimistic while reflecting regarding the future and continuously reminds us to leave the past behind. Leaving the past behind only means possibilities moving forward.

[5] Present Focus

Our futures are important, and we should plan for them, just not focus upon them. The time we should focus and reflect upon is the present day. Do all you can to make each day the best and your future will unfold on its own time.

We have the past, present, and future. Reflecting upon the past is great for returning to our memory banks for special moments and lessons learned. To reflect upon the future is important as well. This is our opportunity to do some planning of the future and maybe even complete a few actions regarding success in getting there. But the future is mostly planning for it because so many things can and will change. The only time to focus upon is now, the present. It is the present that the most impact is possible. Long for the past, be patient for the future, live in the present.

Thoughts and Feelings

There are times in reflection connection that we go from the current moment to distant future; especially when there is much on our minds regarding what yet has come to pass. The problem that exists when we quickly go from present to future that it creates a large gap in time between the two ideas. One thing most important to understand is that moments are right in front of you – don't miss a one. When it comes to distant future – think about it; maybe even reflect upon it, but don't focus on it. Many of us attempt to predict our future by focusing on things that have yet to occur.

Unfortunately, by living this way, we miss the important things right in front of us. It's good to visualize upon the future, but don't miss the important moments that are currently occurring before you.

Think of moments as opportunities. These opportunities are sometimes so quick that we may miss them if we are not completely self-aware as they unfold.

As time is the subject matter of this chapter, then it will be important that you are always self-aware of moments in time while reflecting. If we attempt to live without this awareness, we will miss out on some of the most precious moments of our life.

Response

I believe it is valuable at times to reflect upon the distant future – it's helpful in determining where you want to be and what you need to do to get there – but don't focus on it. Live today first – tomorrow will be here on its own time. I like to think of it as – live for today, not for tomorrow. In other words, first try to understand where you are positioned in today's world and not where you wish you were or where you hope to be someday.

Reflection connection effectiveness is knowing where you are today and understanding that it is more important than where you want to be. Stay focused upon today while reflecting, for tomorrow will be here soon enough. Knowing is also being completely self-aware. It's not easy to be self-aware of all things all the time, but to live a life of reflection connections, you will not want to miss all the important moments of your life as they unfold in the present.

Let's go further. Think and reflect upon this present moment. What are your thoughts? Are you able to stay in the moment? Can you reflect upon what you just read? Or did your thoughts move to 'what's next'? Staying in the present moment is not always easy. It will take practice. No better time than right at this moment.

Lasting Thoughts Regarding Time

Time is one of our most precious commodities, yet it is limited. You could say that we only have so much time. Most of us would say we waste a bit of it, others would admit they would like more of it. Time is still a limited resource. In this chapter we reflected upon time waste, efficiency, challenges, and effectiveness. There will be some time wasted and even occasions of inefficiency, of course some challenges, but the goal should be focusing upon effectiveness.

If our time is indeed this important, then we must improve our efforts regarding how we manage it. We direct the use and how we spend our time. Because we direct these aspects of time, then we can also use it to our advantage. As we think and reflect upon how we use our time, we can be more self-aware and learn to use this limited resource in unlimited ways.

Chapter Ten

Reflective Lessons Learned

As I reflect, what are my most memorable lessons thus far in this life?

In these next [5] reflection connections, the focus is to understand the importance of our lessons learned. Reflections of life's lessons leads us to strong connections resulting in growing towards our potential. It is our lessons that are learned from past experiences that we reflect upon.

Unfortunately, many of our lessons learned were the results of mistakes we made in our past. Many would rather not return to the past because of these experiences in life. What is needed is to humble ourselves and return to the past for guidance of our life today. Reflecting and returning to the past, we may have the opportunity to learn something new regarding what we didn't learn the first time. The past is the past, but you cannot just forget your past. You can attempt, but ultimately you cannot. You can try to push them aside, even pretend they don't exist, but once you have lived these experiences, there they sit until such time you recall and reflect upon past events for lessons that you applied learning – or not. It is the lessons we missed that will continue to appear throughout our life's journey until such time as we fully understand the meaning behind the experiences we had.

It is through these past experiences that we learn from our mistakes as well as successes. Mistakes are intended for us to reflect upon and identify how we can learn by them. Successes are designed for us to reflect upon as well, then repeat for further fulfillment.

Life is meant to be a continuous journey of learning. Lessons are designed to provide us with experiences to move us forward, reaching for our highest potential in life.

As you read this chapter, review each reflection connection and think about those events and situations that will initiate and inspire your own individual reflections that are related to what you read in the examples I have shared. Again, the focus is regarding your reflection connections and the lessons learned by them. To assist you, here are two questions to keep in mind as you read each reflection – (write your own thoughts, feelings, and responses as they resonate with you in the margins of this book. This is your book, your own individual reflection connections, and you should use this book not only as a reference, but as a personal journal of sorts)

1. What can I learn from these reflective experiences?
2. What is the opportunity of growth I can apply from these reflective experiences?

Now, take the journey and discover your own reflection connections throughout this chapter.

[1] Lessons

When I thought about this chapter of reflection connections, it was truly overwhelming regarding the experiences and lessons I have learned thus far in life. Note I write 'thus far'. Life is meant to be a continuous journey of diverse experiences whereas lessons are learned.

Thoughts and Feelings

When we reflect upon lessons, they all provide learning opportunities. It is through these learning opportunities that lead to reflective connection and personal growth. Unfortunately, some people would rather not learn from these lessons. Over the years, many of us have come to realize that we missed some lessons along the way and therefore, we must relive a few mistakes until we learn the meaning intended regarding the lesson. But why not avoid repeating mistakes altogether by learning the lesson the first time? This is a perfect time to reflect. Mistakes are a vital part of life. When we pause and reflect upon them, we can learn not to repeat the same mistakes.

To avoid reliving life's negative situations, we need to change our focus from missing the lesson to understanding why it is a lesson in the first place. If we understand the intended lesson, we can then learn by it and not make the same mistakes in the future. Life's journey is paved with lessons both good and bad. If we reflect upon the lessons from the perspective of both the successes and the failures, we will then heighten our learning experiences. It will be these valuable learning experiences that will define how you live your life.

Response

Even as we age, lessons are still a fundamental part of life. Learning is a continuous process. You should want to learn and never stop being hungry to enhance your knowledge. The consequences if we stop learning in life will be the moment we stop growing. Learning and growing go hand in hand as lessons teach us what we need to know to enhance and improve our lives.

The problem exists when we lump failures with successes producing an 'all is good' mentality, thus creating a no learning atmosphere. When we stop learning in life, we give up our opportunities to continue growing towards our full potential. Unfortunately, many of us will use the self-imposed excuse that we don't want to try anything new believing that if we make mistakes along the way, we won't be successful, so why try? The fact is, in trying something new, most often mistakes will occur. Life is about taking risks, it is part of the lesson of becoming a better, more grounded person. Remember, a failure is not a sign of weakness. Experiencing and learning from our mistakes is a vital part of life for personal growth to occur.

[2] Why?

As the previous reflection connection dealt with lessons, it is these same lessons that happen for a reason. To identify the reason, we must first ask ourselves questions. Lessons are meant for us to question ourselves. During reflecting, the first question many of us turn to is 'why'. The answers to your 'why' will help you with the direction of the lesson you learn from the reflection.

Now armed with answers to your 'why's', you can then decide 'what' to do about it. It is when you learn the lesson that you begin to connect to your reflection.

Thoughts and Feelings

We all have experiences while reflecting in asking ourselves why certain things do not work out. It is a natural response. Unfortunately, many will focus on the negative elements of why things don't always work out. But it is these same negative thoughts and feelings that are the best for lessons to develop into potentially positive results. For some, this is as far as we wish to ponder. This pondering gesture is where we might be most comfortable at stopping. Yet at times, there are others that want to go deeper into the reflection to find answers. Unfortunately, answers are not always available to us. So, no matter how hard we try, the answers to why certain things occur are not to be found.

For those that choose to go deeper while in reflection, this more concentrated effort will cause us to ask more questions of not just why, but how, what, and where. We all do it – it is natural to try to figure things out in our mind, reflect upon, and then to attempt in making sense of it all.

Response

In searching for the answers to questions while reflecting, we will be successful most often in finding the reasons why certain things happen or not. Other times, we are not as successful in identifying the reasons. For those of us who cannot accept that there may be no reason and no definitive answer can feel powerless.

For many of us, finding no reason in our search for answers, can lead to frustration. This frustration emerges and at times, leads to reexamining our questioning to overanalyzing our answers – getting nowhere. It is best to not overanalyze things but to follow our heart, the answer might be stored there. Overanalyzing requires our thinking abilities. If we choose to only use our minds, we may miss the intended connection of the reflection. However, there is another way – understanding the reasons 'why' things happen, requires us to go beyond our mind and consider using our heart.

Why? Because emotions of the heart many times play a stronger role in finding the 'reason why'. The fact is – reasons cannot be identified solely in our minds. It is much more effective to go beyond using just thinking abilities to going deep within our emotions. There are also times we use both thinking and feeling abilities and still do not find the right reasons why something has occurred. It is those times that we exhaust all of our questions that we must let go of finding the actual reasons why things do not always go the way we planned. The reasons, at times, can just be unexplainable. Then there are other times that our questions are answered many years later in life and result in fortunate gifts that were originally labeled as mistakes. Life is truly amazing.

With the emotions of the heart, we can move from just thinking about our reflections, to feeling them deep within. The awesome part about this emotional connection is that we discover some things that can be unexplainable – nothing validated, just accepted for what they are.

If we accept that some things have no specific reason for happening, it can change our thinking with a new perspective of openness and comfort knowing that we exhausted all possibilities.

[3] Mistakes

As stated earlier in the chapter, some of our most valuable lessons learned are from our mistakes. When we reflect upon the 'what' and 'why' of our mistakes, the true lessons begin to surface and are recognized. The wonderful thing about making mistakes are the opportunities to enhance our self-awareness; thus, teach us the 'what' and 'why' of the lessons that are meant for us to learn.

Thoughts and Feelings

Reflection connections will sometimes lead us to remembering our mistakes from the past. This recollection of memories then leads to reflecting upon an expression that many of us are familiar with – 'Show me a person that has learned experiences in the making of mistakes, and I will show you a successful person.' It is from some of our biggest mistakes that can lead us to personal successes. We must also remember that these successes are not automatic, there needs to be lessons learned first.

The key is in the learning. We all make mistakes. The question while reflecting upon our mistakes might be choosing between two different thought processes – do we learn from them and move forward, or to continue to make the same mistakes over and over, creating limitations in life? The choice is for us to make.

Reflection connections allow us to make better choices in the future. If we could change our perspectives regarding making mistakes, it would help us to ultimately reach our most coveted desires – learning from our mistakes the first time and not repeating them.

The fact remains that we are all human beings and we are all going to make mistakes. We can be hard on ourselves or learn from our mistakes to enhance our lives. We choose. Knowing that mistakes are a vital part of life, we can also learn to take risks of doing things differently and then expecting that there will be challenges, or mistakes along the way that will in turn provide valuable learning opportunities.

Response

I believe in responding to making mistakes, we can all say ... 'I have made many mistakes, I have learned from some, and I repeated others.' The ones we learned from; we also grew from. The ones we repeat, we take longer to learn from. Unfortunately, for most of the ones we continue to repeat are self-imposed barriers of simply refusing to acknowledge the mistakes. The mistakes we grow from are designed for us to think differently and admit our mishaps, to learn from them, and then move forward enriched from them – thus the cycle of reflection connection and growth results.

While in reflection our focus should be the benefits regarding making mistakes as they are just temporary setbacks; not permanent. The secret to moving forward from these mishaps lies in what we do to learn from them. Mistakes are never beyond repair. It is while reflecting upon these mishaps that we can change a mistake into positive learning and restore faith in ourselves.

Positive learning is accomplished by finding clarity while reflecting as to why we make mistakes and growing from them afterwards to personally improve as a result.

[4] Choices

It's a fact that life is a series of choices – some good, others are bad. It's interesting that we do learn from both good and bad, but it is from reflecting upon the bad choices that we seem to identify with and learn from the most.

Thoughts and Feelings

When we reflect upon our choices we have made in life, it creates opportunities to learn. It is at this time we also understand that our choices define our life. As we reflect upon and define our life and how we live it, we begin to realize the importance each choice or decision is and the impacts they have upon our life.

Understanding that moment by moment we are making decisions, or choices. It is in these moments that we are self-aware of the possible consequences of those choices. In other words, we make the choices or decisions that are under our direction, but the consequences of those choices are somewhat uncontrolled. It is through our reflection connections that we begin to comprehend just how important our choices define us.

Response

The choices we make define how efficient and effective we are in making decisions. Efficiency and effectiveness are both part of daily life. The true lesson is not just doing something but doing it with your best proficiency.

It is important to make the right choices and understand the consequences. But remember, these consequences are not always under our direction.

There are some negative and many positive consequences to the choices we make. The choices we make in life affect us in many ways. They can affect us negatively or positively. Consequences from these choices can be short or long-term. It is through reflecting upon making good choices and the understanding that these choices must be made at the right time, with the right attitude, and most importantly – for the right reasons.

If choices are made quickly, the consequences or results may not be the desired outcome. It is important to take the time to think, reflect upon, and have a positive attitude – to be effective in doing the right thing. Efficiency can be thought of just as a convenience; whereas effectiveness is more related to completeness. But you still need both efficiency in doing the right thing and effectiveness of doing the right thing right.

[5] Chapters

Earlier we discussed paths and phases in life. Each path, or phase creates a journey. This journey we take is referred to as a chapter in our lives. Some chapters can be longer than others, but a chapter just the same. Reflecting upon our chapters in life creates vivid memories that stay within our hearts for our lifetime.

Thoughts and Feelings

We all reflect upon how we are living life – and – some understand that they can improve it, while others are content with it.

If our intention is to have improvement and to enhance our life, then we must create new chapters. It is exciting to realize that these new chapters will bring additional enhancing experiences and personal growth. So, these new chapters are really nothing more but practice making us more self-aware and highlighting any areas of improvements needed. It is these so-called practice sessions that are the framework of the chapters in our life.

The reference to chapters is of major, long-term events as well as brief situations that occurred for more of a short-lived period. These are the journeys we experience in life. Think about all the chapters that have made us who we are today and the chapters yet to be written. Some chapters we are proud of, while others not so much, but all the same, we cannot avoid them – they are all part of life. In short, life is a continuous book filled with our own individual chapters. It is these chapters of our life that we focus upon while in deep reflection.

Response

The idea that the journey of life is focused upon chapters is a great way to look at it. Our book of life is open, like an incomplete draft and we get to write it. Some of it can be revised, but other parts of the 'book' must be created as new chapters.

We all need to realize that there are many more chapters to be written – and the writing does not stop until we do. Never stop writing new chapters. In fact, a piece of advice – we are all getting older and hopefully wiser. It is from our learned experiences that will help us write the next chapter, and the next, and the next.

Think about the volumes of chapters left to write! It's exciting. Again, recording our life's chapters don't end until we stop the writing.

The past chapters cannot be rewritten, but as we move forward, we can develop and direct how the next chapters are written – which also means we can reflect upon and create the improvements needed along the way, as our life unfolds.

Lasting Thoughts of Lessons Learned

As you reflected upon this chapter, hopefully many thoughts and feelings were inspired by just the mere opportunity of understanding that your life is truly a series of lessons that you have learned thus far. I state thus far because there are many more lessons for you to discover. It is when we continually learn that personal growth begins to take shape.

Along the way, we will make mistakes, have different phases and paths, and we will be asking ourselves several questions; many will be answered, others will not. With the questions that cannot be answered, we have the options of asking more questions or just accepting that there may be no answers – at least right now. If you learned nothing else while reflecting upon these examples, you now have a better understanding and enhanced self-awareness that life is a continuous effort of becoming, and not arriving.

This idea of becoming is the result of all our experiences of lessons learned. In other words, we are always moving forward towards our potential. If you make the extra effort to create new chapters in your own life, it will not only be more exciting, but more meaningful as well.

Chapter Eleven

Reflective Self-Improvements

As I reflect, where have I improved most from my experiences?

In this final chapter, we will go on a journey of [5] reflection connections regarding self-improvement. Are you completely satisfied with your life? How unfortunate is the day for anyone when they believe they are absolutely satisfied with the life they are living, the knowledge they have gained, the achievements they have performed, or the opportunities they created for themselves. Yes, a woeful day indeed that these same most satisfied people never will have the desire to do anything greater that requires seeking further than what they previously believed possible only to stop short of what they were meant and intended to do in life.

The key is to never be satisfied. Always strive for something – anything. Having passion for your purpose in life will motivate you to continue moving forward regardless of any obstacles that present themselves.

It all begins with how you think. If a person changes how they think and reflects upon continuous self-improvement and the consequences of not enhancing their life, would it bring them closer to reaching their full potential and living life differently? The short answer is – yes.

So many things in life can affect our self-improvement. Our attitude, character, passion and purpose are all a part of enrichment. With each experience that we reflect upon, we learn more about ourselves and our purpose. With every situation, we have the opportunity to connect to and see the world from a new perspective.

This new perspective then becomes the foundation to self-improvement. With new perspectives, we also gain enhanced knowledge, or lessons. New perspectives, knowledge, and lessons provide self-improvement opportunities for us.

As in the previous chapter relating to lessons learned, the key is to never stop learning. To think we know it all and that there is nothing more to learn only takes away our desire to continue enriching ourselves. Do not settle for the belief that you 'know it all' – enjoy the learning successes, but then move on to the next opportunity for self-improvement, personal growth, and full potential in life.

As you read this chapter, review each reflection connection and think about those events and situations that will initiate and inspire your own individual reflections that are related to what you read in the examples I have shared. Again, the focus is regarding your reflection connections and how they relate to self-improvements. Hint – the previous chapter was focused upon lessons learned. It is your lessons learned that are meant for the self-improvement areas of your life. To assist you, here are two questions to keep in mind as you read each reflection – (write your own thoughts, feelings, and responses as they resonate with you in the margins of this book.

This is your book, your own individual reflection connections, and you should use this book not only as a reference, but as a personal journal of sorts)

1. What can I learn from these reflective experiences?
2. What is the opportunity of growth I can apply from these reflective experiences?

Now, take the journey and discover your own reflection connections throughout this chapter.

[1] Self-Discipline

If you want to focus upon your self-improvement areas in life, you must be disciplined. Reflections of being disciplined are all about intentional focus and connection. It is when you focus your attention with purpose to connecting to what you need to do, and do it daily, that you will discover self-discipline.

Thoughts and Feelings

If we think and reflect upon the statement: 'You never get what you want; you always get what you deserve' – it makes perfect sense. In other words, if we have discipline and work hard, the results are accomplishment after accomplishment. The key is self-discipline. Think about self-discipline as a habit. This means you do what you need to do without any self-reminders, no one telling you to do it, you just do them – naturally.

Many can reflect upon what they want, but few are willing to say how they are going to get it. Affirmation without self-discipline is fantasy. We never just get what we want; we get what we deserve. Discipline is a habit in which no one achieves and sustains success without it. The key is to stay focused upon the results – the end in mind.

For example, think of a large project that needs to be completed. Anytime we reflect upon the difficulty of the work ahead, rather than on the results or rewards, we are likely to become discouraged. If we dwell on it too long while in reflection, we will develop self-imposed barriers of why we can't complete the work. Then you ask yourself – is it worth the consequences to just give up?

In other words, many of us give up just to be disappointed in ourselves. Why? Because it's easier to not follow through. If we focus on these thoughts while reflecting, the results can create low self-esteem.

Response

When we develop self-discipline while in reflection, the results are stronger, more effective connections. Having self-discipline is hard work. Self-discipline requires extra efforts of passion and enthusiasm. You can accomplish anything if you make discipline a habit in life. If we are disciplined in everything we do, we will achieve positive results – the next promotion at work, good grades in school, in our relationships, at the fitness center, for a new business venture, etc. It is those extra efforts that will bring greater successes in life.

What does it take to have self-discipline? It is when faced with insurmountable odds against us to get things done, that our focus may reflect upon the thoughts of giving in or giving up; but our self-discipline rises above to continue moving forward regardless of how we may think or feel. This type of reflection connection is what separates being good from being great. For any accomplishment to be fulfilled, if we do not have self-discipline, we will not be as successful. Self-discipline is the key in reaching our maximum potential in life. For those that possess this self-discipline, know and understand just how important it is to put into daily practice. For what you practice daily, creates habit and this habit becomes a natural occurrence day after day that pushes you forward no matter the barriers that stand before you.

[2] Questions & Answers

In a previous chapter I shared the idea of asking the question – 'why'. This reflection connection goes further into asking questions connected to our self-improvement efforts. Hopefully questions you ask yourself while in reflection connection will eventually lead you to the answers you are seeking. To reach the right answers, you must first ask the right questions.

Thoughts and Feelings

Many times, while reflecting, we are searching for answers regarding why certain situations have occurred in the past. What if we search for answers and cannot find them? The wonderful thing about finding the answers or not, self-improvement exists – it is in the search or the experience itself where growth takes place.

So many of us struggle with finding the right answers to questions arising from reflections of events and situations in life that it affects the way we see the world. How many times have you asked yourself 'why' certain things have happened (or not) and did not find the right answers? Unfortunately, many will search for the answers that may never come. Why is this? It might be that we are not asking the right questions. When we ask ourselves questions in reflection, unless we are completely focused, the right questions will not materialize. Self-improvement is all about knowing when to ask the most effective questions to find the right answers.

Response

How many of us have searched for answers to situations that have occurred in life only to end up frustrated after searching and coming up empty?

What we need to learn is focusing our efforts upon finding answers while reflecting, but not linger. Even after asking the right questions, we may still have difficulty in finding the right answers. We can remain frustrated or we can simply move forward knowing that we did our best to find the answers. Isn't that all we can ask of ourselves?

We may just need to accept that sometimes the right answers will not be there. Try to find them, but if they don't come in a reasonable amount of reflection concentration, move forward anyway. What we need to realize is some questions we have regarding life simply cannot be answered. To continue to be frustrated, disappointed, and confused by not finding the right answers only will damage us emotionally.

We need to do our best to reflect upon and attempt to find the right answers to life's many questions. There may be no straightforward answers, but there will always be self-improvement areas discovered during this process.

As we continue to ask questions, and finding most answers, we are enhancing our lives. It is self-awareness that works alongside self-improvement. We may not find all the answers, but we can always improve our lives.

[3] Overthinking

Overthinking or overanalyzing anything will only bring about more stress. By focusing upon what we want and why will simplify any process.

Regarding self-improvement, our reflections should focus on 'what' we want to improve on, and the 'whys' will come with taking effective steps forward. It is healthy to reflect upon the 'what' because the 'what' answers 'why' you are doing something in the first place. Keep it simple.

Thoughts and Feelings

When we reflect upon self-improvement, we can sometimes overthink our goals for moving forward in life. It is when we overthink or overanalyze the experiences of our lives, that these goals become more confusing.

There is another option. Understanding that our minds can be overfilled with too much information, why not consider our emotions, or a feeling from the heart? We get so consumed with analyzing our goals that we don't take the necessary steps to move forward. It is when we involve our heart and the emotional side of our reflections, that we begin to identify what prevents us from moving forward and understand what we need to do.

Every reflection involves some type of thinking, but it is when we tend to overthink that we get confused, frustrated, and unsure of what actions to take. By doing this, it clouds our minds so much that we cannot move forward in life. What's missing? Our heart. What is our heart telling us?

Response

The important thing to do while reflecting is to keep it simple. To keep improving your life, simply develop a plan for self-improvement. One that is direct and easy to follow – what and why.

The results of keeping things straightforward is understanding what we need to do in the simplest of terms, thus making life less complicated and more importantly, less stressful.

Using the emotions of our heart while reflecting, will provide us more perspective than just thinking about it. When we involve our emotions while reflecting to any part of the decision-making process, we then think and more importantly, feel the possibilities of deciding the best alternative in the process.

When we think and reflect, we need to feel deeply within to experience and connect to the full perspective of whatever event or situation we are faced with. Feelings come from our heart – we need both mind and heart to work together while reflecting for clarity to be successful dealing with life's situations.

[4] Character

Anytime we reflect upon our own individual self, we will often times pause and think about what our current character is. If our focus is embracing growth, our reflections will then seek to improving it. Life is a continuous series of learning, improving, and growing. When we take the necessary efforts to improve ourselves, we build upon our character.

Thoughts and Feelings

When reflecting upon improving our lives, it is oneself that should be focused on first. Our character is vitally important while attempting to improve upon our lives.

During such times as we make efforts to improve, we also make mistakes along the way. Fortunately, it is through our experiences of making mistakes that much learning takes place. While the learning takes place, it is also when our character gets tested regarding the difficulty of the lessons learned. It is also in these difficult times that we can falter, resulting in damaging our character. Although looking at a different perspective, it is times such as faltering in life that we will feel less than perfect. But we do have choices. We can bury our character deep within or we can choose to build upon our character.

When we make the choice to bury our feelings, we then have the perception that all regrets in life are mistakes. It is at this moment that we must deeply focus and reflect upon facing our fears regarding our mistakes and move forward despite these self-imposed barriers. Every time we face mistakes and attempt to move forward despite them, it creates a test of our character. Our tested character can be best described as actions we take regarding life's most difficult events. Character is created within through reflecting upon ourselves and shown by our actions on the outside. These actions will clearly demonstrate just how strong of a character we possess.

Response

This is life and mistakes are a big part of it. It is times such as these that our true character is tested. Giving in or giving up should never be an option. To achieve excellence in life takes forward reflective thinking and effort. This is no ordinary thinking nor effort. It is purposeful thinking and exceptional effort.

There may be times in life when giving in is the easier path to take, but our character on the inside will make us stand tall on the outside. It is when we continue to stand tall no matter the circumstances that we can develop deeper self-confidence to enrich and enhance our lives.

There always comes a time when giving up seems easier than standing up, when giving in looks more appealing than our own strong-will. And it is in these moments that our true character may be the only thing we have to draw on to keep us moving forward in life. A tested character is how we react to life's situations. Depending on how we reflect upon our character and then respond regarding actions that need to be taken, will many times define us as an achiever or a quitter in life.

[5] Confident Beliefs

Many beliefs we have in ourselves can be very encouraging, other beliefs – not so much. It is those 'other beliefs' that we must focus upon while in reflection to improve ourselves. One important belief is our confidence level. Confidence is a belief that must be built. There is nothing like having confidence in yourself and the abilities that you possess within.

Thoughts and Feelings

Reflecting allows us to create certain beliefs within. It is our belief regarding ourselves that leads to our own level of elevating our lives. It's quite simple, we can enhance ourselves to move forward in life or we can remain in the same place. It's how we feel internally. In this case, there is only positive or negative. You choose.

Any internal belief regarding our abilities is a choice we develop within. With a strong heart and faith in our abilities, we can accomplish what we want in life. Internal belief starts with reflecting and connecting to what we think. Once we have a strong belief in our abilities, we can then begin the process of personal growth.

To get started, it's always best to think and reflect upon confidence regarding our personal growth. Confidence is essential. A strong sense of self is usually built upon many experiences that we are proud of and have considered them successes. Confidence starts with believing in ourselves – our capabilities, strengths, and natural talents. A strong heart and mental toughness are the foundation needed to be confident in oneself.

Response

If we adopt a positive attitude while reflecting, we create the confidence necessary for continued successes in life. It starts with believing in ourselves and the choices we make. We need to develop the continuous habit of reflecting and connecting to past choices we have made and learn the lessons intended from them. Once we embrace these lessons each day with confidence, they will go a long way to create future successes and self-improvement. Embracing this foundation, each time we attempt and then accomplish what we want to complete, our confidence grows along with our joy and happiness.

The best way to experience confidence is to begin with a positive attitude. Going into any situation with a positive attitude will increase your confidence level. Confidence is not something you just automatically possess; it must be built.

This confidence is built through reflecting upon it and believing in yourself. Once this confidence is built, it must be sustained for continued growth opportunities. As you continue to experience different situations and create positive results, your confidence grows. Each time your confidence grows, you have the opportunity to sustain it.

Lasting Thoughts Regarding Self-Improvement

Every reflection connection begins with a thought. If you want to improve yourself, your thoughts will lead you to what things you want and need regarding enhancing your life. Thoughts are only the beginning of the process. To create self-improvement opportunities in your life, you must take the appropriate actions.

As we reflect upon how to improve ourselves, we can suppress our feelings about them, or we can take the necessary actions to become the best we can be. It all comes down to choices. The choices we make are ours alone to follow-through in creating a life-long commitment to improving ourselves. Each day we make choices while reflecting to improve our circumstances or remain the same. Take advantage of each day to learn something new and when you do, you will move closer to your full potential in life.

Chapter Twelve - One Step Further

How to Turn Responses into Personal Potential

After reading the various chapters of reflection connections in this book, hopefully you have discovered that it is purposeful reflection connections that allow us to expand upon a deeper sense of introspection in shaping our thoughts, inspiring and stretching our feelings, and initiating natural responses to promote better self-awareness. If this improved self-awareness is then embraced and applied to learning, that leads us to personal growth which in turn produces enrichment in our lives.

It is through our effective responses that begin the true connection to our reflections. When we effectively create our own reflection connections, we then begin to increase both mental and spiritual introspection for overall self-improvement.

So, why not go one step further?

There is more work to do. As purposeful reflection connections go, I intentionally added the last two chapters regarding lessons learned, followed by self-improvement to help you move to the next step: personal potential. Learning unlocks your potential. Self-improvement moves you from how good you currently are, to how great you could be.

In other words, the embracing of diverse learning and the pure act of self-improvement goes deeper, or one step further, to complete the connection to your reflections. This book focuses upon our purposeful thoughts and feelings; immediately followed by responses. Having intentional thoughts and feelings while reflecting is only the start of the self-awareness process. It is the effective actions you take after your reflections that connection and growth begin to take shape. Growth begins with actions. It is these actions that will lead you to your own personal potential.

All throughout the book I have asked the same two questions at the beginning of each chapter for you to focus upon and answer as you reviewed my reflection connection examples:

1. What can I learn from these reflective experiences?
2. What is the opportunity of growth I can apply from these reflective experiences?

First learning, then growth is applied to move us closer to our personal potential and fulfillment. If you are like most, the responses to reflections will seem almost automatic, or natural. Learning starts with responding. Responding is the foundation to connection.

In this chapter, we will briefly go beyond simple responses to effective actions you can initiate to move towards your personal potential. Note that I state initiate. You are the only one that can direct this kind of influence upon yourself. Hopefully, the previous two chapters regarding lessons learned and self-improvement have already inspired you to take the next steps, or actions to personal potential.

In reflecting, many people do not recognize the value that once they have reflected upon thoughts and feelings regarding their experiences, they must go further into reflection to create effective actions. Not understanding this great opportunity and potential for personal growth is unfortunate. Another way to think about it is that although we may reflect upon life experiences, and maybe even recognizing some of the potential benefits, we don't go any further to realize the true lessons within these experiences. This, of course, resulting in no follow-through with actions to actually grow from the reflective experiences.

The true value of reflection connections is to take actions after you have deeply thought about the potential learning that come from past experiences. With learning comes self-improvement; thus, increasing your personal potential.

When purposefully reflecting, you must understand that every thought and feeling has the possibility to go to the next level and be applied in a way that personal potential can be maximized.

Going Deeper with Personal Insights

Going deeper into reflection turns each experience into personal insight. It is personal insights that prompt us to take effective actions we need to initiate moving us from simple self-awareness to personal potential. The goal moving forward is to release the powerful thoughts and feelings of our reflections and attaching them to actions to reach personal potential. This process starts by unlocking our thoughts and feelings to strive for our best in life. Personal potential is your own individual best efforts to being more than you have already become – making your best better.

It's personal because it's about you and your passion to fulfilling your true potential – a purposeful achievement to enrich your life.

Personal insight begins with a personal commitment to initiate these four effective actions daily:

1. Make an appointment – with yourself

Each morning set aside time to make an appointment with yourself to reflect. Start with the previous days' both successes and mistakes. The successes, you want to continue to repeat each day. The mistakes are for improved self-awareness to embrace learning to be applied from your reflections.

It's unfortunate that most people fear mistakes more than they want to learn by them, but when you learn from your difficult experiences, you can apply encouraging actions leading to your personal potential.

You may also reflect upon any past events where learning could be initiated. With learning comes actions to apply towards self-improvement areas to enhance your life. When reflecting daily, we choose from past experiences to present day. Be sure to make and keep this important appointment daily.

2. Think to yourself

Strong thinking starts with going deep within and deciding what you need and want to change while reflecting. Again, it is effective actions that must be initiated to reach full personal potential. Remember that all actions will begin with your thoughts.

Now your thoughts move to creating responses as to what needs to change. These changes are initiated from the first action of reflecting upon your previous days' events or something from the past.

As we get closer to responses, actions flood our minds. These actions many times are from new perspectives regarding our reflections. The newly discovered reflective experiences will prompt us to respond in some way. It is these responses that lead to unproven actions we will need to take.

We must be aware of unproven actions that can also cause undue pressures. Rather than hiding from these pressures, rise from them. As a result, you don't let pressure define you. When you release any pressure that you may feel, it then provides you with an open mind and heart to create better outcomes from your reflections.

To produce better outcomes, thoughts of asking yourself a series of questions are essential. These questions must be answered before moving into actions. While reflecting considering what actions to take, thoughts go from asking yourself the question:

- What can I learn from these reflective experiences?

To then asking:

- What is the opportunity of growth that I can apply from these reflective experiences?

Remember, you will have had the opportunity to practice answering these two questions as they were part of each chapters' introduction.

Along the way, I am sure there was some doubt in answering these questions. Doubt leads to fears. It would not be uncommon to discover some fears that you may have experienced of reading the examples of reflection connections I shared in this book. It is how you responded when you experienced these fears that is the key. To reach your personal potential, you must learn to understand and release your fears.

To do this, you must ask yourself more questions.

Then ask yourself questions such as these:

- o How can I face my fears?
- o Not just letting go of my fears but, what can these experiences teach me?

Then lastly –

- o How can I implement the teachings of this book into my life to encourage more self-awareness while reflecting upon my experiences?

3. Talking to yourself

When you reflect, you are talking to yourself. These are the most important conversations you can have to create connections to your reflections. Self-talk has potential to have great impacts on us. In these self-conversations, we can choose to stay positive even if it's a negative experience you are reflecting upon. Remember that it all begins with what and how we think, and we can change what and how we think.

Focus upon reminding yourself that these reflections are for better self-awareness to apply beneficial learning from your mistakes and that each reflection gets you closer to becoming the person that you were created to be.

4. From talking to writing

As you have now made an appointment with yourself, inspired your thoughts, and initiated self-talk; it's time to write down your intentions. When you take this time to write, you are beginning to connect to your reflections.

As suggested, writing your own individual thoughts, feelings, and responses in the margins of the book as you review the reflections would not only inspire you, but you will create your own reflection connections to the readings. The thoughts and feelings from your reflections must be recorded in some way as so you don't forget them. You will not have a clear direction unless you can state your actions in writing.

Further, writing makes you think things through. When you then write down your intentions, again you will want to answer a series of questions before moving to potential actions. In other words, it forces you to think about and record all your options and perspectives before moving forward with demonstrated actions.

Once you have answered all your questions, now write down your actions. It is now time to be accountable, or to own your intended actions. When you own something, it motivates you to get results. By owning your outcomes, you are investing in your own individual growth. The more accountability and responsibility you invest in yourself, the closer you move to personal potential.

Moving forward ...

Taking in account for all four of these effective actions regarding personal insights, we can then take the necessary steps to embrace and apply learning from our reflective experiences, moving us closer to our own individual personal potential.

This book may end, but your work is unfinished. This book is only to inspire you to reflect through your thoughts, feelings, and some natural responses. You now can take the next steps to fully connect and further enhance and enrich your life.

The only way to achieve your desires and dreams is to act upon them. The greater you trust in yourself, your beliefs, and your thoughts, the more actions you will take. Now take the necessary time to put your actions to work to move you closer to fulfillment and personal potential.

ABOUT THE AUTHOR

Gary is the founder of Conflict Coaching Solutions, LLC, a professional life coaching business that focuses on inspiring individuals, couples, and/or groups to transform their conflictive situations into positive solutions.

Before creating his company, Gary was a "corporate coach" for a large utility company in Southern California. During his 32 years with this company, Gary designed and developed several coaching courses and workshops that he facilitated to supervisors and managers throughout the company.

Gary has a Bachelor of Science degree in Organizational Management and a Master of Science in Leadership and Management.

Gary also has previously written and published three other books; The Coach's Chronicles Trilogy. For additional information regarding Gary and his business or books, go to: conflictcoachingsolutions.com

Made in the USA
Lexington, KY
14 November 2019

57044735R00083